10 Minute Guide to Lotus® 1-2-3® Release 2.3

Katherine Murray

Doug Sabotin

SAMS

A Division of Macmillan Computer Publishing
11711 North College, Carmel, Indiana 46032 USA

To Doug—
*Because whether it's football or music (**right, Bobby?**)*
or writing, being There is all there is.

katie

©1991 by SAMS

FIRST EDITION
FIRST PRINTING—1991

International Standard Book Number: 0-672-22809-2
Library of Congress Catalog Card Number: 91-61041

Publishing Manager: *Marie Butler-Knight*
Managing Editor: *Marjorie Hopper*
Development Editor: *Lisa Bucki*
Manuscript Editor: *Charles Hutchinson*
Book Design: *Dan Armstrong, reVisions Plus, Inc.*
Cover Design: *Dan Armstrong*
Production: *Brad Chinn, Denny Hager, Bruce Steed*
Indexer: *Jill D. Bomaster*
Technical Reviewer: *San Dee Phillips*

Printed in the United States of America.

Trademarks

Contents

Introduction

Perhaps you walked into work this morning and found a Lotus 1-2-3 Release 2.3 package sitting beside your computer, along with a new mouse. Until now, all you've heard about 1-2-3 is that it allows users to create spreadsheets for performing calculations and graphs for displaying numeric data as effectively as possible. A few things are certain. You need:

- To navigate 1-2-3 quickly and easily.

- To identify and learn the tasks necessary to accomplish your particular needs.

- Some clear-cut, plain-English help to learn the basic features of the program.

Welcome to the *10 Minute Guide to Lotus 1-2-3 Release 2.3*. Because most people don't have the luxury of sitting down uninterrupted for hours at a time to learn a new program, the *10 Minute Guide* teaches the operations you need in lessons that you can complete in 10 minutes or less. The 10-minute format offers information in bite-sized, easy-to-follow modules, it lets you stop and start as often as you like because each lesson is a self-contained series of steps.

What Is the *10 Minute Guide?*

The *10 Minute Guide* series is a new approach to learning computer programs. Instead of trying to teach you everything about a particular software product (and ending up with an 800-page book in the process), the *10 Minute Guide* covers the most often-used features in 20 to 30 short lessons.

The *10 Minute Guide* teaches you about programs without relying on computerese or technical jargon—you'll find only simple English used to explain the procedures in this book. With straightforward, easy-to-follow steps and special artwork, called *icons*, to call your attention to important tips and definitions, the *10 Minute Guide* makes learning a new software program quick and easy.

The following icons help you find your way around in the *10 Minute Guide to Lotus 1-2-3 Release 2.3*:

Timesaver Tips offering short-cuts and hints for using the program more effectively.

Plain English definitions of new terms.

Panic Button problem areas—how to identify them and how to solve them.

A "Table of Features" and a "Table of Functions" at the end of the book provide you with a quick guide to 1-2-3 features and functions not fully covered in this book. A

"DOS Primer" introduces often-used DOS commands and procedures.

Specific conventions are used to help you find your way around 1-2-3 as easily as possible:

Numbered steps	Step-by-step instructions are highlighted so that you can easily find the procedures you need to perform basic 1-2-3 operations.
What you type	The keys you press and the information you type are printed in bold type and a second color.
Menu names	The names of menus, commands, buttons, and dialog boxes are shown with the first letter capitalized for easy recognition.
Menu selections	The options you select from the 1-2-3 menus are also printed in bold type and a second color.

The *10-Minute Guide to Lotus 1-2-3 Release 2.3* has 23 lessons, ranging from basic startup to more advanced graphing features. Remember that nothing in this book is difficult. Most users want to start at the beginning of the book with the lesson on starting 1-2-3, and progress (as time allows) through the lessons sequentially.

Who Should Use This Guide?

The *10 Minute Guide to Lotus 1-2-3 Release 2.3* is for anyone who

- Needs to learn 1-2-3 quickly.

- Feels overwhelmed by the complexity of 1-2-3.

- Wants to find out quickly whether 1-2-3 will meet his or her computer needs.

- Wants a clear, concise guide to the most important features of the 1-2-3 program.

What's New with Release 2.3?

Lotus 1-2-3, Release 2.3, offers features earlier versions of 1-2-3 did not possess. These new enhancements include:

- Dialog boxes that pop up over the spreadsheet, allowing you to select options easily without interrupting your work (see Lesson 3).

- A Wysiwyg ("What-you-see-is-what-you-get") feature that allows you to produce professional-looking graphs and spreadsheets (see Lesson 16).

- An auditing feature that helps you analyze the formulas in your worksheet and locate errors (see Lesson 9).

- A new file viewing capability that lets you see the contents of files without actually retrieving them (see Lesson 7).

For Further Reference, Consult...

The First Book of Lotus 1-2-3 Release 2.3, Second Edition, by Alan Simpson and Paul Lichtman

The Best Book of Lotus 1-2-3 Release 2.3, Fourth Edition, by Alan Simpson and Paul Lichtman

Lesson 1
Starting
Lotus 1-2-3

In this lesson you'll learn how to start Lotus 1-2-3.

Before you begin working in Lotus 1-2-3, you must have already installed the program on your system. Make sure that you have installed it correctly. This 1-2-3 installation program asks for information about the various screens, printers, and drivers that are associated with your computer. Providing this information will allow you to work more efficiently in Lotus 1-2-3. (See the inside front cover for installation instructions.)

Starting Lotus 1-2-3 with a Hard Disk

To start Lotus 1-2-3 on a hard disk system, follow these steps:

1. Make sure the DOS prompt displays the drive on which you have installed 1-2-3. With a hard disk, this should be either C: or D:.

2. To get to the Lotus directory, type **CD\123R23** and press Enter. This directory is where you installed the information necessary for 1-2-3 to run properly.

1

3. Type **123** and press Enter. You will see a copyright screen for a brief moment, and then the work area will appear, as shown in Figure 1-1.

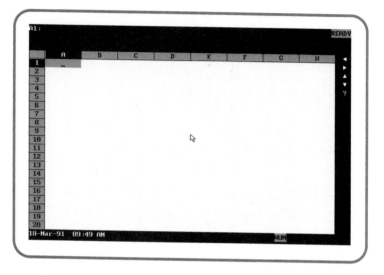

Figure 1-1. The initial work area in Lotus 1-2-3.

Starting Lotus 1-2-3 without a Hard Disk

If you are working on a computer that doesn't have a hard disk, you can start Lotus 1-2-3 by following these steps:

1. Put the DOS Startup disk in the appropriate drive and close the drive door. Then turn on your computer.

2. Get to the DOS prompt. The prompt will look like A : > or A> (or B : > or B>).

3. Take the DOS Startup disk out of the drive and put in the 1-2-3 system disk.

4. Type **A:** and press Enter to initialize the 1-2-3 system disk. If the drive isn't A:, make sure you type in the appropriate drive letter followed by a colon.

5. Type **123** and press Enter. You will see a copyright screen for a brief moment, and then the initial work area will appear (again see Figure 1-1).

What If 1-2-3 Didn't Start?

In most cases 1-2-3 will start without any problem. There is a chance, however, that after you follow the previous steps, 1-2-3 will not start. If this happens, you will see an error message such as Bad command or filename.

Before you go back to the installation process, make sure that you have followed the steps for starting Lotus 1-2-3 correctly. If, after going back through the steps, you reach the same error message, refer to the installation of 1-2-3 outlined on the inside front cover of this book to make sure you have installed Lotus 1-2-3 correctly.

Turning on Wysiwyg

All the figures in this book were created with 1-2-3 in Wysiwyg mode. To turn on the wysiwyg feature, select **/A**dd-In **A**ttach and then select **WYSIWYG.ADN**. Then press Enter twice. For more information about Wysiwyg, see Lesson 16.

In this lesson you've learned how to start Lotus 1-2-3 using a hard disk and non-hard disk system. In the next lesson you'll explore the Lotus work area.

Lesson 2
Exploring the Lotus Screen

In this lesson you'll learn about the basic elements of the Lotus 1-2-3 screen.

Elements of the Lotus Screen

The 1-2-3 screen contains all the elements—menus, commands, work area, and mode indicators—you need in order to work with 1-2-3. Figure 2-1 shows a typical 1-2-3 screen. (You can display this screen by pressing /.)

Work Area

The work area of the screen is perhaps the most obvious of its elements. Organized in columns and rows, like a sheet of columnar paper from an accountant's pad, the work area helps you organize and work with the data in your worksheets.

Cell In any spreadsheet program, a cell is the intersection of one column and row. For example, cell C6 is the intersection of column C and row 6.

4

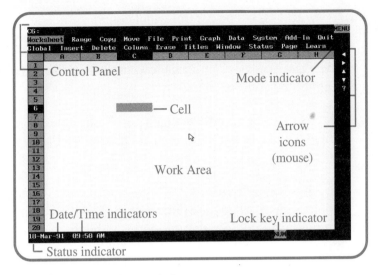

Figure 2-1. The 1-2-3 screen.

Across the top of the work area you see a highlighted line that helps you identify which column the cursor is in. There are 256 columns, lettered from A to IV. The left edge of the work area is bordered by another highlighted line, this one numbering the rows of the worksheet, from 1 to 8,192.

> **Reading Cell Addresses** When you are referring to a cell, you list the column first, and then the row. For example, if you are referring to the fourth cell in column E, you would write that cell address as E4.

Although the spreadsheet extends all the way to IV8192, only cells through H20 are shown on the initial screen.

Control Panel

The control panel appears at the top of the 1-2-3 screen. In the control panel, you choose menus and commands to

5

interact with 1-2-3. The control panel contains three lines that tell you the following things:

- The first line gives information about the currently highlighted cell.

- The second line shows the characters being entered or edited, or, when the Main menu is activated, it shows the Main menu.

- The third line provides a description of the command being used, or, when the Main menu is active, it lists the options available for the currently highlighted command.

Look at the control panel in Figure 2-1. The first line shows the address of the cell and displays the formula that is currently being stored in that cell. The second line shows the Main menu, and the third line shows the options available for the highlighted **W**orksheet command.

Mode Indicators

The mode indicators appear in the upper right corner of the 1-2-3 screen. Table 2-1 lists the modes available in 1-2-3 and provides a brief description of each.

Table 2-1. Mode Indicators.

Mode	Description
EDIT	The contents of a cell are being edited.
ERROR	A formula or operation causes an error; press Esc or Enter to remove the ERROR indicator.
FILES	You need to select a file name.
FIND	A database operation is being performed.

Mode	Description
HELP	A help screen is displayed.
LABEL	You are entering a label.
POINT	You are pointing to a range.
NAMES	You need to select a range name from a displayed list.
MENU	You are selecting a menu option.
READY	The program is waiting for a cell entry or command.
VALUE	You are entering a number or formula.
WAIT	1-2-3 is processing a command.

Lock Key Indicators

The lock key indicators are displayed in the lower right corner of the screen. Most keyboards have lock keys—such as Scroll Lock, Num Lock, and Caps Lock—which act as toggles; that is, you press the key once to turn on the feature and press the key again to turn it off. When you press one of these keys, 1-2-3 displays an indicator reminding you of active keys (CAPS for Caps Lock, END for End, OVR for Ins, NUM for Num Lock, and SCROLL for Scroll Lock).

Status Indicators

The last type of indicators used by the 1-2-3 spreadsheet are status indicators. These indicators tell you the type of operation 1-2-3 is performing, or let you know when an error has occurred, and tell you what type of error it is (see Table 2-2).

Removing Error Messages To remove a status indicator error and return the spreadsheet to READY mode, press Esc or Enter.

Table 2-2. Status Indicators.

Indicator	Description
CALC	The worksheet needs to be recalculated.
CIRC	There is a circular reference error.
CMD	A macro or Command Language program is running.
MEM	1-2-3 is running out of RAM space in which to save the worksheet.
SST	A macro or Command Language program is running in step-by-step mode.
STAT	The status of the worksheet is being displayed.
STEP	You are stepping through a macro or Command Language program.

Using the Keyboard

Now that you know the basics of the 1-2-3 screen, you need to know how to use the keyboard to move around the display. Table 2-3 lists the keys you'll use to move the cursor (also called the *cell pointer*) in the worksheet area.

Table 2-3. Keys for Moving the Cursor.

Key	Function
↓	Moves cursor down one row.

Key	Function
↑	Moves cursor up one row.
→	Moves cursor right one cell or to next command or option.
←	Moves cursor left one cell or to next command or option.
Tab	Moves cursor right one screen.
Shift-Tab	Moves cursor left one screen.

Try the following examples:

1. Press the ↓ key four times. (The cursor moves to cell A5.)

2. Press the → key twice. (The cursor moves to C5.)

3. Press Tab. (The entire display is scrolled to the right one screen. The cursor is positioned in cell I5.)

4. Press Shift-Tab. (The display is returned to the earlier display, with the cursor in cell A5.)

There are other keys that are important to your use of 1-2-3 as well. A brief description of each of these keys is shown in Table 2-4.

Table 2-4. Other Important Keys in 1-2-3.

Key	Description
/ (slash)	Displays the 1-2-3 Main menu.
Backspace	Erases most recently entered data.

(continued)

Table 2-4. (continued)

Key	Description
Esc	Removes menu or cancels error message.
Enter	Places value or text in cell, or selects command or option.
F1 (Help)	Accesses help.
F2 (Edit)	Turns on EDIT mode.
F3 (Name)	Displays list of range names for current worksheet.
F4 (Abs)	Makes a relative cell address an absolute or mixed address (more about this in Lesson 10).
F5 (GoTo)	Moves cell pointer to the cell address you specify.

Try the following example:

1. Press F1. 1-2-3 displays the Help screen.

2. Press Esc to return to the worksheet display.

Using the Mouse

Lotus 1-2-3 Release 2.3 adds the capability of working with the mouse as you select options from the menu system. Following are a few terms you should be familiar with if you are using a mouse:

Point	Move the mouse until the cell or menu option you want is highlighted.

Click   When you have highlighted the cell or
            option you want, press and release the
            mouse button.

Drag   Position the mouse at the point you want
            to begin highlighting; then press and
            hold the mouse button while you move
            the mouse to highlight the entire group
            of cells you want to select.

To select menu options by using the mouse:

1. Display the Main menu by pressing / (slash).

2. Point to the menu option you want to select.

3. Click the mouse button.

Or

1. Display the Main menu.

2. Click on the arrow icons at the right edge of the screen
   to move the highlight to the option you want.

3. Click the mouse button.

Getting Help You can access the 1-2-3 Help
screen by using the mouse to point to the ? icon
on the right side of the screen and clicking the
mouse button. You can choose the topic related
to the operation you are performing. At this
point, you also have the option of selecting
Index to display a list of available help topics.

Exiting 1-2-3 If you want to exit 1-2-3 at this
point, press / and select **Quit** from the Main menu.
Highlight **Y**es and press Enter when you are
asked to confirm that you want to leave the
program.

Lesson 3
Using Menus and Dialog Boxes

In this lesson you'll learn how to use the menu system and dialog boxes in Lotus 1-2-3.

Introducing the Menu

The Main menu contains the commands you'll use as you work in Lotus 1-2-3. Table 3-1 explains them.

Table 3-1. Commands in the Main menu.

Command	Description
Worksheet	Contains the commands that affect the entire worksheet.
Range	Includes commands used to select and work with a range of cells.
Copy	Enables you to copy a cell or range of cells.
Move	Enables you to move a cell or range of cells.
File	Allows you to perform various file maintenance operations.

Command	Description
Print	Enables you to print a range or an entire worksheet.
Graph	Helps you choose settings for a graph that you need to be create or modify.
Data	Allows you to work with the database features of 1-2-3.
System	Closes 1-2-3 temporarily and opens the operating system.
Add-in	Enables you to work with add-in programs.
Quit	Ends the current work session.

Opening the Main Menu

Before you can use the menu, you must first open it. To do this, follow these steps:

1. Make sure that the worksheet you are working on is in READY mode. The word READY should appear in the top right corner of the screen.

2. Press the / (slash) key to open the Main menu in the control panel (see Figure 3-1).

   Using the Slash Key Don't confuse the slash (/) key with the backslash (\) key. If you press \ (backslash) by mistake, press Esc (or Backspace) and you will return to the original screen; then press / (slash) and the menu will appear.

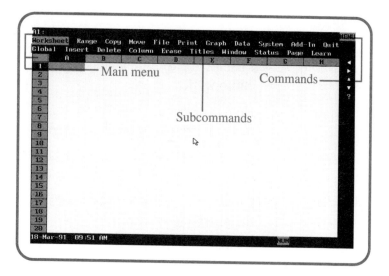

Figure 3-1. The Main menu in the control panel.

Figure 3-1 shows the commands available in the Main menu. The second line of commands lists the subcommands available after you select a command on the first line. As you move the highlight from command to command, the bottom line changes to show you the additional commands that are available.

Selecting a Command

To move through and select a command in the Main menu, use the following steps:

1. After you open the Main menu, use the ← and → keys to move through the list until the command you need is highlighted.

2. Press Enter.

Moving through the Command List You can move the highlight to the beginning or end of the command list by pressing Home or End.

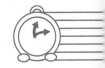

Selecting a Command Quickly choose a command from the Main menu by pressing the first letter of the command you want.

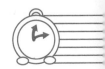

A few of the commands in the Main menu do not have subcommands, such as Copy. In this case, after you highlight the command, the line underneath the Main menu displays a description of what the command will do if selected.

What If I Select the Wrong Command? If you accidentally choose the wrong command or subcommand, press Esc on the keyboard. Lotus will take you back to the previous step.

After you have selected a command and the subcommand line appears at the top of the control panel, you can move through the list in the same manner described earlier. As you move through the subcommand list, the second line provides you with a description of what each highlighted option will do if chosen.

Entering Information After Selecting a Command

n some instances, after you select a command you must type in information that will allow you to continue. Try the following example:

1. From the Main menu, move the highlight to the File menu name.

2. Press Enter.

3. Highlight the Save command, which is used to save a worksheet you've created.

4. Press Enter. You will be shown a list of all the files currently saved in 1-2-3. Assume the worksheet you have created is a new one.

5. Press Esc. You will see a message in the control panel similar to the following: `Enter name of file to save:`

6. Use the appropriate keys to delete and type in the file name for the worksheet.

7. Press Enter.

8. To return to the Main menu, press Esc repeatedly until the Main menu appears on-screen.

Using Dialog Boxes

Lotus 1-2-3 Release 2.3 introduces a new feature that makes 1-2-3 easier to use: *dialog boxes*. Dialog boxes pop up over your worksheet to show you a set of options available for the operation you are performing. For example, Figure 3-2 shows a dialog box displayed when you select /Worksheet Global Format.

Dialog Box Elements

Dialog boxes contain several different elements that help you make selections. Table 3-2 lists the various elements and provides a brief description of each.

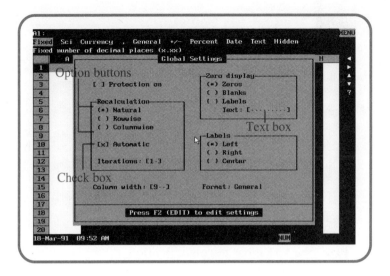

Figure 3-2. Example of a dialog box.

Table 3-2. Dialog Box Elements.

Element	Description
Option buttons	Use to select individual settings (as in the Recalculation column, Natural).
Check boxes	Use to select one or more items in a list of options.
Text boxes	Use to type in a specific setting.
List boxes	Use to choose from a list of displayed options.
Command buttons	Use to carry out the dialog box operation (usually OK or Cancel).

Making Dialog Box Selections

When you want to select an item in a dialog box, follow these steps using the keyboard:

1. Press F2.

2. Press Tab until the option group you want is high-lighted.

3. Use the arrow keys to move the highlight to the option you want.

4. Press the space bar to select the item.

 Selecting Dialog Box Options Quickly After you display the dialog box and press F2, press the first letter in the option name to select it.

 Mouse Selection When a dialog box is open, click on any option with the mouse to select it.

Lesson 4
Entering Data

In this lesson you'll enter data and begin creating your worksheet.

Planning the Worksheet

Before you begin creating worksheets on your own, you'll want to consider what type of data you'll be working with. Think about the information and decide which data should be placed in columns and which should be placed in rows.

For example, suppose that the owners of ABC Bakery want to find out which of their products made the most money. For a three-month period they kept separate totals for their catering, walk-in, and special-order customers. At the end of that time, they used 1-2-3 to analyze the results.

In planning the worksheet, they realized that each of the three months—January, February, and March—should occupy a column, and the three totals—Catering, Walk-In, and Special Order—should occupy rows. Figure 4-1 shows the completed worksheet.

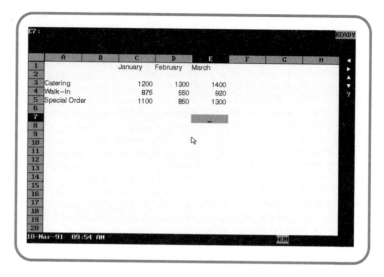

Figure 4-1. The sample worksheet.

Entering Labels

After you've decided on how you want to organize the worksheet, you need to enter labels. (You cannot enter data when the Main menu is displayed, however. If the Main menu is showing, press Esc to return to the worksheet.) For most worksheets, you'll want to enter both column and row labels. For this example, do the column labels first.

Adding Column Labels

To add column labels, type the labels, pressing → after each entry. For example, follow these steps:

1. Starting in cell A1, press the → key twice to move to cell C1.

2. In C1, type **January**. Press the → key.

3. In D1, type **February**. Press the → key again.

4. In E1, type **March**. Press →.

Adding Row Labels

Row labels extend down a column of the worksheet (usually the first column, A). To add row labels, type the labels, pressing ↓ after each entry. For example, follow these steps:

1. Start in cell A1. Press the ↓ key twice to move to cell A3.

2. In A3, type **Catering**. Press ↓.

3. In A4, type **Walk-In**. Press ↓.

4. In A5, type **Special Order**. Press ↓.

Figure 4-2 shows the worksheet with the column and row labels entered.

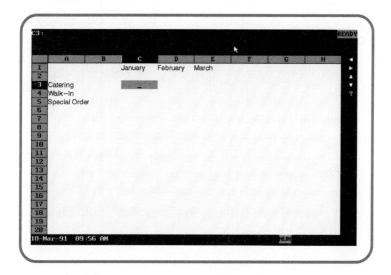

Figure 4-2. The labels in the worksheet.

Lengthy Labels If you enter a label that is longer than the column is wide, 1-2-3 displays the label by using part of the next cell, if no information is currently entered in that cell. You may want to change the width of the column to display the entire label without infringing on subsequent cells. (Lesson 13 explains how to change column width.)

Aligning Labels 1-2-3 also gives you the option of aligning the labels in your worksheet by centering, right-aligning, or left-aligning the labels. Lesson 14 explains more about working with the label format.

Entering Values

After you enter the labels in the worksheet, you're ready to enter the values. Use the same technique you used for entering labels. Type the entry and then use an arrow key to accept your entry and move to another cell. For example, follow these steps:

1. Use the arrow keys to move the cell pointer to cell C3.

2. In C3, type **1200** and press the → key.

3. In D3, type **1300** and press the → key.

4. In E3, type **1400** and press the ↓ key.

5. Press the ← key twice to move the cell pointer back to cell C4.

6. In C4, type **875** and press the → key.

7. In D4, type **550** and press the → key.

8. In E4, type **920** and press the ↓ key.

9. Press the ← key twice.

10. In C5, type **1100** and press →.

11. In D5, type **850** and press →.

12. In E5, type **1300** and press the ↓ key.

Your sample worksheet should now resemble the one shown in Figure 4-1.

Now you know how to create a basic worksheet. Before you can really analyze anything, of course, you need to be able to perform calculations on the worksheet values. In later lessons you'll learn how to use functions and formulas to work with the data you've entered in this lesson.

In this lesson you've learned how to enter labels and data into a worksheet. In the next lesson you'll learn how to save the sample worksheet you've created.

Saving the Worksheet and Exiting 1-2-3

In this lesson you'll learn how to save your work and exit 1-2-3.

Saving a Worksheet

When you create a worksheet in 1-2-3, the program temporarily saves the work in its memory. After you have finished a work session or have made significant changes to a worksheet, you need to save your work. Saving a worksheet stores it permanently on a floppy or hard disk. This procedure ensures that you can get back to this worksheet in the future if necessary.

There are a few rules you should keep in mind when you save a worksheet. The file name

- Can be up to eight characters long.

- Cannot contain any blank spaces.

- Must contain only letters, numbers, and underscore (_) or hyphen (-) characters.

Saving a New Worksheet

To save a newly created worksheet in 1-2-3:

1. Make sure that the program is in READY mode. (The word READY will appear in the top right corner of the screen.)

2. Press / (slash) to activate the Main menu.

3. Press → until the **F**ile command is highlighted.

4. Press Enter.

5. Press → until the **S**ave command is highlighted.

6. Press Enter. Line 3 of the control panel shows a horizontal list of the files saved in 1-2-3, similar to the one shown in Figure 5-1.

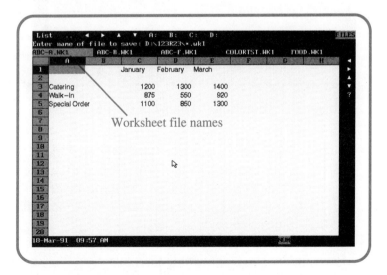

Figure 5-1. The list of files saved in 1-2-3.

Selecting Commands Quickly You can quickly select a command by pressing the first letter of the command when the Main menu is displayed.

7. To activate the default file name line so that you can enter your own file name, press Esc. You should see a flashing cursor preceded by the directory that the file will be saved in, as shown in Figure 5-2.

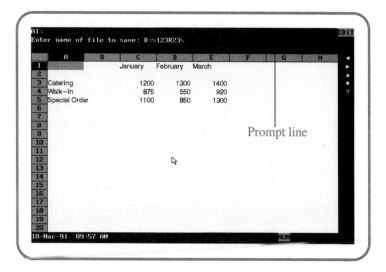

Figure 5-2. Entering the name of the file to save.

8. If this is the directory you want to save your worksheet in, type in the appropriate file name. If not, backspace over the default directory and type in the directory and file name you would like to use. (Name the sample file **ABC-A.WK1**.)

9. Press Enter. The document is then saved.

Saving a Modified Worksheet

Occasionally, you must modify a file that you have saved previously. In this case, you can save the worksheet in one of two ways:

- As a new worksheet with a new file name.

- As an updated version of the same worksheet (with the same file name).

If you want to save the modified worksheet with a new file name, follow the steps for saving a new worksheet (described in the previous section). To save a worksheet with the file name it was last saved under, follow these steps:

1. From READY mode, press / (slash) to activate the Main menu.

2. Use → or the mouse to highlight the File command.

3. Press Enter.

4. Use → or the mouse to highlight the Save command.

5. Press Enter.

6. 1-2-3 shows you the existing file name in the control panel. Press Enter, and the document will be saved in its current form.

7. After you press Enter to save the modified worksheet with the same name, you can do one of three things:

   - Cancel the command, which will leave the existing file in memory.

- Replace the existing file with the modified version.

- Back up the new file by giving the old version of the worksheet a BAK extension. This choice will save both files with the same name but different extensions.

8. Use → or the mouse to highlight the command you need.

9. Press Enter. This will save your worksheet according to the choice that you have made.

Exiting 1-2-3

After you have finished working in 1-2-3 and have saved the work you have done, you need to know how to exit 1-2-3. To get back to the DOS prompt, follow these steps:

1. From READY mode, press / (slash) to activate the Main menu.

2. Press End to highlight the Quit command.

3. Press Enter. 1-2-3 prompts you to end your 1-2-3 session in the control panel.

4. Use → or the mouse to highlight Yes.

5. Press Enter. You will return to the DOS prompt.

Saving Your Work If you have been working in 1-2-3 and have not saved your work, the program gives you one last chance to save it before exiting. To save the worksheet, select No at the prompt to exit 1-2-3, which returns you to the worksheet so that you can save it. You can then exit the program as usual.

Lesson 6
Retrieving a Worksheet

In this lesson you'll learn how to retrieve a saved worksheet.

Retrieving a Worksheet

After working in 1-2-3 for some time, you will accumulate a list of different worksheets that you have created and saved throughout your work sessions. You will probably need to go back into these files more than once.

Losing the Current Worksheet When you retrieve a worksheet, the new worksheet automatically erases the worksheet on-screen. Make sure that you have saved your current worksheet before you retrieve any other.

To retrieve a worksheet that you have saved, follow these steps:

1. From the READY mode, press /(slash) on the keyboard to activate the Main menu.

2. Press → key until the File command is highlighted, or use the mouse to highlight the command. Press Enter.

3. Highlight the **R**etrieve command.

4. Press Enter. 1-2-3 displays a horizontal list of the available files, as shown in Figure 6-1.

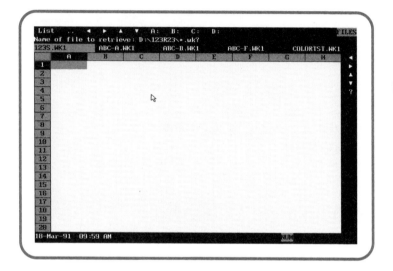

Figure 6-1. The **R**etrieve command dialog area.

5. Move through the list of files using the arrow keys until the file you need is highlighted. Or, if you know the file name of the worksheet, press Esc and the `Name of file to retrieve:` prompt will appear. Then you can type in the file name.

6. Press Enter.

Displaying a List of Files

Rather than scrolling through the horizontal list of file names displayed in the control panel, you can display a full-screen list.

Use the mouse to point to the List indicator in the top left corner of the screen and then click the mouse button. 1-2-3 automatically highlights the List indicator when you select **/F**ile **R**etrieve. If you are using the keyboard, you can select List simply by pressing Enter. The spreadsheet disappears, and you see a full-screen list of files in the current directory (see Figure 6-2).

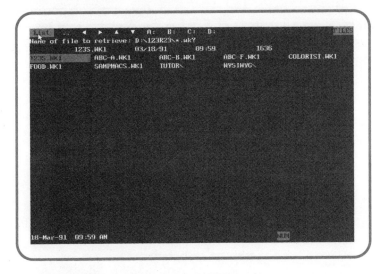

Figure 6-2. Using the List feature to show directory contents.

Select the file you want by clicking on the name of the file in the displayed list or by using the arrow keys to highlight the file you want and then pressing Enter.

Undoing the Retrieve

If you retrieve a saved worksheet and have forgotten to save your previous work or need to get back to it, you can return to the previous worksheet as long as you have not begun working on the retrieved file. To get back to the previous worksheet, follow these steps:

1. Make sure that the UNDO indicator appears in the status line of the work area, as shown in Figure 6-3.

2. Press Alt+F4 to return to the previous worksheet.

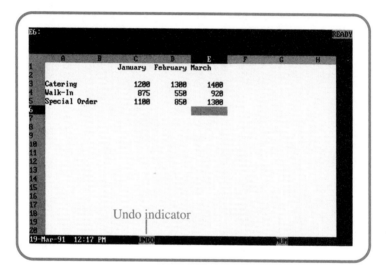

Figure 6-3. The UNDO feature in Lotus 1-2-3.

If UNDO Isn't Displayed If UNDO does not appear in the status line, turn the UNDO feature on by selecting /Worksheet Global Default Other Undo Enable and then choosing /Worksheet Default Other Update.

In this lesson you've learned to retrieve a worksheet and undo the retrieval. In the next lesson you learn about 1-2-3's add-in programs.

Using 1-2-3's Add-In Programs

In this lesson you'll find out how to load the add-in programs included with 1-2-3 Release 2.3.

What Are Add-Ins?

An add-in program is a special utility that adds to the capabilities of 1-2-3 while you are using the program. 1-2-3 Release 2.3 includes five different add-in programs:

- Wysiwyg, a new program that allows you to see your spreadsheet on-screen the way it will appear in print.

- Tutorial, a step-by-step program that leads you through the basics of using Release 2.3.

- Spreadsheet Auditor, a new feature that allows you to examine and check the formulas in your worksheet.

- Viewer, a program that lets you view the contents of spreadsheet, database, and text files without retrieving them into 1-2-3.

- Macro Library Manager, a feature that stores important items—such as macros, ranges, and formulas—which you use repeatedly in different spreadsheets.

Attaching Add-ins

Before you can use one of the add-in programs, you must load the program (this is known as *attaching* the add-in). To attach an add-in, follow these steps:

1. Press / (slash) to display the Main menu.

2. Select Add-In.

3. Select Attach. 1-2-3 lists the add-ins (see Figure 7-1).

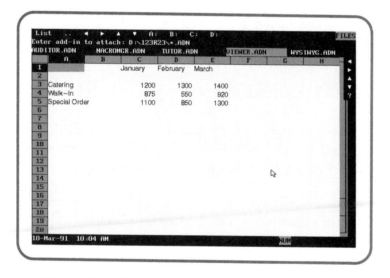

Figure 7-1. Selecting an add-in.

4. Highlight the name of the add-in you want to use. (For example, choose **VIEWER.ADN**.)

5. Press Enter. 1-2-3 gives you the option of assigning the add-in to a specific key so you can start the program with a single keystroke. For now, leave **No Key** highlighted.

6. Press Enter again. 1-2-3 then attaches the add-in so that you can use it as necessary.

Invoking Add-Ins

When you are ready to use the add-in program you've selected, you need to use the /Add-In Invoke command to start the program. Try the following example:

1. Press / (slash) to display the Main menu.

2. Select Add-In.

3. Select Invoke.

4. Choose the add-in from the list of available add-in programs. (For example, choose VIEWER.ADN.)

5. Press Enter. The add-in is then ready to use.

Using an Add-In (Viewer) and Its Options

The Viewer feature is an add-in program that allows you to look at the contents of a file without actually retrieving the file into your worksheet. You can also use Viewer to link files and browse through 1-2-3, Symphony, or text files.

First, attach and invoke Viewer, if you haven't already done so, using the steps in the preceding sections. When the Viewer screen is displayed, you can Retrieve, Link, or Browse through files within Viewer (see Figure 7-2).

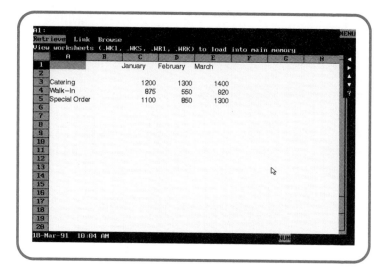

Figure 7-2. Selecting Viewer options.

To display the Viewer screen, select **R**etrieve. The screen shown in Figure 7-3 is then displayed. The left side of the Viewer screen displays a list of files in the current directory; the right side shows the current worksheet. If you want to see what's in one of the files in the left column, follow these steps:

1. Use the arrow keys or the mouse to move the highlight to the file you want to view.

2. Press Enter or click the mouse button. The contents of the file are displayed on the right side of the Viewer screen.

You cannot, however, edit or modify the file in any way. Viewer simply allows you to see what the file contains before you actually retrieve the file. If you do want to retrieve the file, return to 1-2-3 by pressing Esc twice and use the **/F**ile **R**etrieve command as usual.

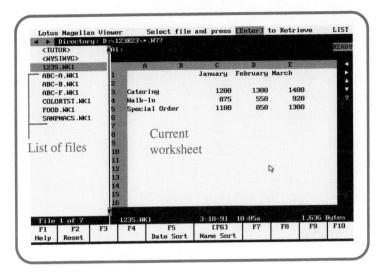

Figure 7-3. The Viewer screen.

Removing an Add-In

To remove an add-in from memory, follow these steps:

1. From within 1-2-3, press / (slash).

2. Select Add-In.

3. Select Detach.

4. Choose the add-in name (for example, **VIEWER.ADN**). The add-in is then released from memory.

In this lesson you've learned how to attach, invoke, use, and release 1-2-3's add-in programs. In the next lesson you'll learn how to work with ranges in your worksheet.

Lesson 8
Working with Ranges

In this lesson you'll learn to select, work with, and name ranges in your worksheet.

Why Use Ranges?

The term *range* in 1-2-3 refers to a range of cells. While some operations you perform affect the entire worksheet (such as some global formatting commands), for other operations you need to highlight a range. You'll use ranges, for example, when you want to do the following tasks:

- Copy a column or row of numbers to another part of the worksheet.

- Total a column or row of numbers.

- Delete a section of the worksheet.

- Change the format for a portion of the worksheet.

- Move a block of cells.

For many operations in which you'll be specifying ranges—such as copying or moving a block of cells—

1-2-3 prompts you to enter a range. In other cases, such as when you are entering a range in a formula, you must decide when you want to enter a range.

> **Range** A range is any rectangular block of cells you highlight to perform certain operations.

Selecting a Range

In 1-2-3, a range can be as small as one cell or as large as the entire worksheet. You can select a range three different ways, by

- Typing the cell addresses for the range.

- Using the cell pointer or directional arrows to point to the range.

- Entering a name you've already assigned to the range.

Typing Cell Addresses

First, retrieve the example spreadsheet you've been using thus far. Then try the following copy procedure to learn how to type a range when 1-2-3 prompts you to. To start the procedure, follow these steps:

1. Position the cell pointer on cell C3.

2. Display the Main menu by typing / (slash).

3. Use → or the mouse to move the highlight to Copy.

4. Press Enter. In the control panel, 1-2-3 asks you to Copy what? (see Figure 8-1).

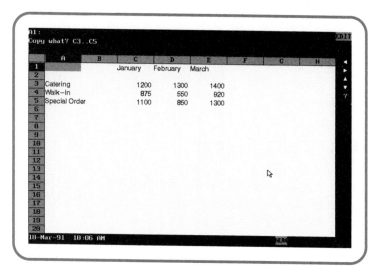

Figure 8-1. The prompt to enter a range for a copy procedure, with a range specified.

5. Backspace through the default values 1-2-3 displays.

6. Type the cell address where you want the range to start (in this case, C3).

7. Type two periods (..)

8. Type the cell address that marks the place you want the range to end (in this case, E5). The range you specified looks like C3..E5, as shown in Figure 8-1.

9. After you press Enter, 1-2-3 continues with the copy procedure and asks you to provide another range indicating where you want to place the copy. For now, back out of the copy procedure by pressing Esc until you return to the worksheet in READY mode.

Pointing to a Range

Try the same basic procedure to illustrate pointing to a range. Repeat steps 1 to 4 of the preceding copy procedure. Then point to the range following these steps:

1. Use ↓ to highlight cells C3 through C5.

2. Press → until all cells through E5 are highlighted.

3. Press Enter.

When you press Enter, 1-2-3 automatically enters the range you pointed to and continues with the copy procedure, asking you to specify the point on the worksheet where you want to place the copy.

If you are using a mouse, you can point to the range by following these steps:

1. Point to cell C3.

2. Press the mouse button.

3. Drag the mouse until cells C3..E5 are highlighted.

4. Release the mouse button.

Deselecting Ranges To deselect a range, press Esc or move the mouse pointer away from the selected range and click the mouse button.

Naming Ranges

If you use certain ranges repeatedly in your spreadsheet, you may want to assign a name to the range so that you don't

41

have to use the pointing or typing methods each time you need to specify a range. For this reason, 1-2-3 allows you to assign a range name to any range you use often.

Assigning a Range Name

To assign a range name to a block of cells, follow these steps:

1. Press / (slash) to display the Main menu.

2. Press → to select the **R**ange command.

3. Press Enter.

4. Select the **N**ame option by highlighting the option and pressing Enter or by typing **N**.

5. Select the **C**reate option by highlighting the option and pressing Enter or by typing **C**.

6. When 1-2-3 prompts you to Enter name:, type the range name you want (for the sample worksheet, type **JANSALES**) and press Enter (see Figure 8-2).

7. Select the range you want to name by either pointing to or typing the range addresses (for this example, choose cells C3..C5).

8. Press Enter. 1-2-3 assigns the range name to the cell range you specified.

Selecting a Range by Using the Range Name

To see how to use a range name when you're asked to specify a range, try this example:

1. Press / (slash) to display the Main menu.

2. Select Copy.

3. At the `Enter range to copy FROM` prompt, type **JANSALES.**

4. Press Enter. 1-2-3 accepts that range as the range you want to copy from and continues the copy operation, asking you where you want to place the copy. Again, press Esc to back out of the copy operation.

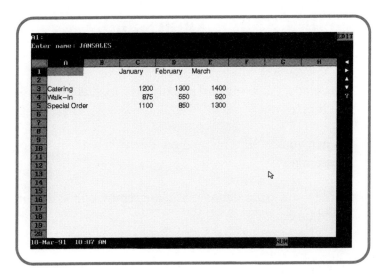

Figure 8-2. Assigning a name to a range of cells.

Displaying Range Names

Remembering range names you've created may be easy if you've used only one or two in your worksheet, but what happens when you've named 15 or 20 different ranges? 1-2-3 gives you the capability to display a list of range names so that you can choose the one you need. To display the range names for the current worksheet:

1. Start an operation that prompts you for a range (you can use the copy procedure for an example, if you choose).

2. When 1-2-3 is in POINT mode (shown in the indicator at the top right corner of the screen), press F3 (Names).

1-2-3 displays a list of range names in the bottom line of the control panel. Scroll through the list using the arrow keys until the range name you want is highlighted; then press Enter to select the range.

Deleting Range Names and Erasing Ranges

At first glance, deleting and erasing may look the same. In 1-2-3, they're not.

- When you *delete* a range, you are deleting the name of the range.

- When you *erase* a range, you are removing the data in the range.

Deleting a Range

When you want to delete a range name, follow these steps:

1. Display the Main menu by pressing / (slash).

2. Choose the Range command.

3. Select Name.

4. Select Delete.

5. From the list of displayed range names, highlight the name you want to delete.

6. Press Enter. 1-2-3 then deletes the range name you assigned to that range of cells.

Erasing a Range

There will be times when you want to erase a portion of the worksheet. To erase a range, follow these steps:

1. Display the Main menu by pressing / (slash).

2. Choose the Range command.

3. Select Erase.

4. When 1-2-3 asks for the range to be erased, enter the range name, or type or point to the cell range.

5. Press Enter. 1-2-3 erases the contents of the cells in the range you specified.

Lesson 9
Using Formulas and Functions

In this lesson you'll learn to add formulas to your worksheet.

What Is a Formula?

Put simply, a *formula* is an equation in 1-2-3. A formula can be as simple as 1+1 or as complicated as a complex equation to figure out a logarithmic value. You'll use formulas in 1-2-3 when you want to perform a vast number of operations, such as

- Finding the total of a group of numbers.

- Determining the average of a range of cells.

- Performing statistical analyses on groups of numbers.

- Creating a "what-if" analysis based on changing numeric factors.

1-2-3 provides you with a set of special functions that can perform different tasks for you. Many of the formulas you create may include functions, but using a function in a formula is not mandatory.

Entering a Formula

For this lesson you'll start with a basic formula that doesn't include a function. The next section shows you how to use functions.

Suppose that, using the spreadsheet example set up in earlier lessons, you want to add the values in cells D3 through D5 and place the result in cell D7. To do this, follow these steps:

1. Load the sample worksheet.

2. Use the arrow keys or the mouse to move the cell pointer to cell D7.

3. Press +. 1-2-3 formulas must begin with a number or one of the following symbols: + − @ . (or $.

4. Type **D3+D4+D5**.

5. Press Enter. 1-2-3 calculates the result and displays it in cell D7 (see Figure 9-1). Line 1 of the control panel displays the formula.

Using Operators in Formulas

Operators tell 1-2-3 how to work with the values in the formula. The operators allowed in 1-2-3 formulas are shown in Table 9-1.

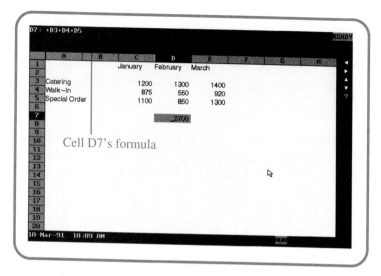

Figure 9-1. Using a formula to total a column.

Table 9-1. Operators Used in Formulas.

Operator	Description
+	Addition (or positive)
–	Subtraction (or negative)
*	Multiplication
/	Division
^	Exponentiation

You also use parentheses to show how you want 1-2-3 to carry out the execution of the formula. For example, consider the simple formula

4–3+2

If you place parentheses around the first two values so that the formula reads (4–3)+2, the result is 3. However, if you place the parentheses around the second two values so that the formula reads 4–3+2), then the result is –1.

If Your Formula Doesn't Work If you get an error when you try to enter a formula, check to make sure that (1) you have entered a closing parenthesis for each opening parenthesis; and (2) you haven't inadvertently entered a comma in the wrong place.

Using Functions in Formulas

1-2-3 comes with a set of preset functions you can use in your worksheet. (These functions are explained in more detail in a table of functions included at the back of this book.) Begin all 1-2-3 functions with an @ sign and enter them in capital letters.

For example, you could total a column of values by using the @SUM function. Try the following example:

1. Load the sample worksheet.

2. Use the arrow keys to move the cell pointer to cell C7.

3. Type @SUM(.

4. Enter the range of cells you want to total by pointing to the range, typing the range, or entering a range name. (In this case, enter JANSALES, because we named that range in Lesson 8.)

5. Type the closing parenthesis.

6. Press Enter. 1-2-3 places the result in cell C7 (see Figure 9-2). The control panel displays the function.

49

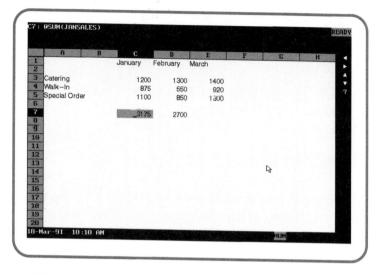

Figure 9-2. The result of using a function in formula.

Thinking Ahead At this point, save your sample worksheet, (ABC-A.WK1) so you can return to it later. Lesson 5 explains saving procedures.

Editing a Formula

Inevitably, you'll want to edit formulas and data in your worksheet after you enter them. 1-2-3 makes this easy, as in the following steps:

1. Place the cell pointer on the cell containing the formula you want to edit.

2. Press F2 (Edit).

3. Press the Backspace key to back up over the necessary characters.

4. Retype the correct characters.

5. Press Enter. 1-2-3 completes the change, and the worksheet is placed back in READY mode.

Displaying Formulas

Although usually you'll want to work with the regular display of 1-2-3, the program gives you the option of displaying all the formulas you've created in their appropriate cells. To show the formulas in the worksheet, follow these steps:

1. Display the Main menu by pressing / (slash).

2. Choose the Worksheet command.

3. Select the Global option.

4. Choose the Format option.

5. Choose the Text option. 1-2-3 displays all the formulas in the appropriate cells on-screen (see Figure 9-3).

Note that the entire formulas are not displayed because the column width is too narrow. You learn to widen columns in Lesson 13.

> **Returning to Normal Display** Change the formulas back into values by selecting /Worksheet Global Format General.

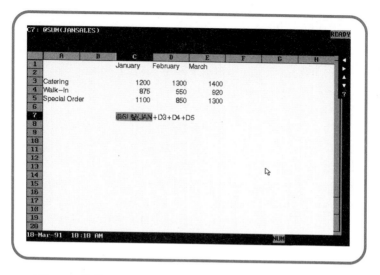

Figure 9-3. Displaying formulas in the worksheet.

Using the Auditor

Lotus 1-2-3 Release 2.3 includes an add-in program called the Spreadsheet Auditor that allows you to examine and error-check all the formulas in your spreadsheet.

The Auditor can help you

* Determine which cells depend on a particular formula.

* Find all formulas on the worksheet.

* Locate any circular references.

* Show all formulas in order of calculation precedence.

The Auditor is an add-in program, which means you use it while you are working with 1-2-3. Because the Auditor uses memory, you won't want to keep the Auditor loaded at all times.

52

When you invoke the Auditor, 1-2-3 displays the Auditor Settings dialog box (see Figure 9-4).

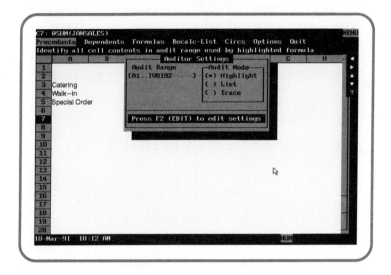

Figure 9-4. The Auditor Settings screen.

To edit the options, press F2. Press **M**. Choose one of the following audit modes, and then press Enter:

- Options Highlight, which highlights the cells found.

- Options List, which lists the cells.

- Options Trace, which lets you examine each cell individually.

Press **R** and type an Audit Range. Then press Enter twice.

Use the arrow keys to select the Auditor operation. Press Enter. Type a source cell, if Auditor asks for one. Press Enter. Auditor performs the operation you requested. Table 9-2 lists the options and brief descriptions of each.

Table 9-2. Auditor Operations.

Option	Description
Precedents	Finds all cells referred to in formulas in a specified range.
Dependents	Finds dependent cells to the formulas in a range.
Formulas	Locates all formulas in a range.
Recalc-List	Identifies formulas in their order of calculation.
Circs	Finds all circular references.
Options	Sets options for range or mode of audit.
Quit	Returns you to 1-2-3.

When you are ready to detach the Auditor from memory, follow these steps:

1. Press / (slash).

2. Select Add-In.

3. Choose Detach.

4. Select AUDITOR from the list and press Enter.

Lesson 10
Copying and Moving Cells

In this lesson you'll learn various methods for copying and moving cells.

Understanding Relative and Absolute Cell Referencing

In an earlier lesson you learned how to read a cell's address. There's another aspect to cell addressing that you need to know before you copy or move cells in your worksheet. 1-2-3 gives you the option of assigning cells absolute or relative addresses when you *reference* (specify) the cells in a formula.

By default, all cell references in formulas are *relative*. If you move or copy a formula with relative cell addresses, the formula's cell addresses change to reflect the formula's new place in the worksheet. When you assign a cell an *absolute* address in a formula, the address of the cell will not change when you move or copy the formula.

Consider this example. The formula +C3(C5–D5) in cell D6, contains relative addresses. The contents of D5 are subtracted from C5, and then the result is multiplied by the contents of C3. If C3=5, C5=8, and D5=2, then the result is 30.

If you copy the formula to another location, the cell references (and, therefore, the contents of the cells) change. Suppose that you copy the formula to M20, which is nine cells down and 14 cells right of D6. The formula now reads L17(L19–M19). Each cell address in the copied formula is nine cells down and 14 cells right of the corresponding address in the original formula. You simply copied the formula, but 1-2-3 automatically adjusted the cell addresses so that the correct values would be used in the formula: L17=4, L19=6, and M19=4. The result is 8.

When you assign absolute addresses in a formula, the cell references do not change. Therefore, the formula would remain the same no matter where on the worksheet you placed the copied formula. (If the formula contains some relative and some absolute references, only the relative references change to reflect the new location.)

To assign an absolute address to a cell, enter a dollar sign ($) before both the column and row of the cell address, such as **+C3(C5–D5)**.

To create an absolute address for a cell, you can:

• Type the dollar signs in the appropriate places as you enter the formula.

• Press F4 (Abs) at the place in the formula you want 1-2-3 to add the dollar signs for you.

Before you copy or move cells, be sure to examine the formulas in your worksheet to see whether you need to assign any absolute addresses.

Mixed Addressing 1-2-3 also allows you to create a mixed address, which mixes absolute and relative addressing. See *The First Book of Lotus 1-2-3, Release 2.3, Second Edition.*

Copying Cells

With 1-2-3, you use the Copy command to copy a cell or a range of cells. You have four options for the type of copy operation you can perform:

- You can make a copy of one cell.

- You can copy one cell into many cells.

- You can make a copy of a range of cells.

- You can copy one range to a larger range of cells.

To copy cells, follow these steps:

1. Return to the sample worksheet.

2. Display the Main menu by pressing / (slash).

3. Select the Copy command (see Figure 10-1).

4. When the Copy what? prompt appears, if you are copying a single cell, position the cell pointer on that cell, or type the cell address. If you are copying a range of cells, point to or type in the range of cells you want to copy. (For this example, type C3..C5 after the prompt.)

5. Press Enter.

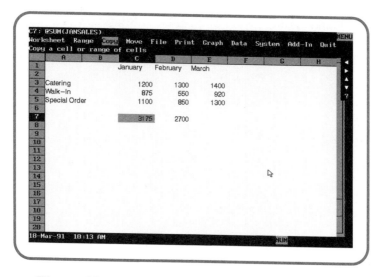

Figure 10-1. Choosing the Copy command.

6. The To where? prompt appears.

- If you are copying a single cell to another single cell, place the pointer on that cell, or type the address.

- If you are copying a range of cells to a range of the same size, position the cell pointer at the beginning cell of the range where you want to place the copy, or type that cell's address. (For this example, move the pointer to F10.)

- If you are copying a single cell or a range of cells and placing the copy into a larger range—for example, suppose you want to copy C3..C5 to a larger block of the worksheet such as F10..H20—either type the range of cells you want to receive the copy, or highlight the range you want to copy to.

7. Press Enter. 1-2-3 then copies the range of cells you specified (see Figure 10-2). Any formulas included in

58

that range are also copied and automatically modified to reflect their new placement.

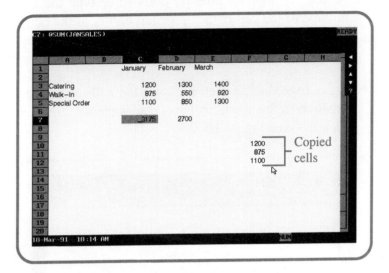

Figure 10-2. The completed copy procedure.

Moving Cells

The move procedure is similar to the copy procedure. Instead of placing a duplicate of a cell or a range of cells at another point in the worksheet, however, 1-2-3 moves the cells to another location.

To move cells, follow these steps:

1. Display the Main menu by pressing / (slash).

2. Select the Move command.

3. At the Move what? prompt, point to or type the address of the cell or range of cells you want to move. For this example, type **D3..D5**.

4. Press Enter.

5. At the To where? prompt, point to or type the cell address of the cell in the upper left corner of the range where you want to place the moved cells. (For this example, position the cell pointer on cell D10.)

6. Press Enter. 1-2-3 then removes the cells from their position in the worksheet and places them at the new location (see Figure 10-3).

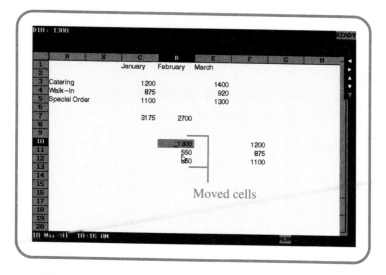

Figure 10-3. Moving worksheet cells.

Returning to the Old Worksheet Return to a previously saved version of the worksheet by using **/**File **R**etrieve.

In this lesson you've learned about relative and absolute cell addressing and found out how to copy and move cells. In the next lesson you'll learn how to edit the contents of cells and delete cells you no longer need.

Lesson 11
Editing and Deleting Cells

In this lesson you'll learn how to edit cell contents and delete unneeded cells. You'll also learn about manual and automatic recalculation.

Editing Cells

Editing is easy with 1-2-3. Simply place the cell pointer on the cell you want to modify and then press F2 to change 1-2-3 into EDIT mode. The contents of the cell appear in the display panel. Then you can use a variety of keys to edit the contents of the cell as necessary (see Table 11-1).

Table 11-1. Editing Keys in EDIT Mode.

Key	Action
Esc	Removes all characters in edit line.
Del	Deletes character at cursor position.
Backspace	Removes character to the left of the cursor.
Ins	Changes between INSERT and OVERTYPE modes.

(continued)

61

Table 11-1. (continued)

Key	Action
→	Moves cursor one character to the right in edit line.
←	Moves cursor one character to the left in edit line.
Tab	Moves cursor five characters right.
Shift-Tab	Moves cursor five characters left.
Ctrl-→	Moves cursor five characters right.
Ctrl-←	Moves cursor five characters left.
Home	Moves cursor to beginning of edit line.
End	Moves cursor to end of edit line.

To edit a cell, follow these steps:

1. Position the cell pointer on the cell you want to edit.

2. Press F2 (Edit). 1-2-3 displays the EDIT indicator in the upper right corner (see Figure 11-1).

3. Edit the cell as necessary (using the keys in Table 11-1).

4. Press Enter. 1-2-3 then records your changes and returns the worksheet to READY mode.

No Forwarding Address... When you edit cell formulas, remember whether the cell addresses should be relative or absolute. If you edit a formula that contains absolute addresses and forget to reassign the absolute cells (see Lesson 10), you may wind up with unexpected—and erroneous—results.

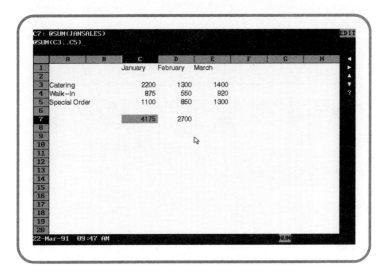

Figure 11-1. Editing worksheet cells.

Setting Recalculation

Any time you edit information on your worksheet, you will undoubtedly find formulas that need to be recalculated. You can have 1-2-3 automatically recalculate your worksheet for you after any change or addition (this is known as *automatic recalculation*), or you can have the program recalculate the spreadsheet only when you specify (known as *manual recalculation*). The 1-2-3 default is automatic recalculation.

To change to manual recalculation, follow these steps:

1. Display the Main menu by pressing / (slash).

2. Choose the Worksheet command.

3. Select Global.

4. Select Recalculation.

63

5. Choose Manual (see Figure 11-2).

6. Press Enter.

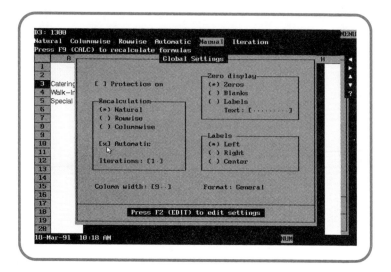

Figure 11-2. Choosing manual recalculation.

When you return to the worksheet, 1-2-3 will recalculate the spreadsheet only when you press F9 (Calc). If, at a later time, you want to change back to automatic recalculation, repeat steps 1 through 4 and then choose Automatic instead of Manual.

Deleting Cells

To erase the contents of a single cell, follow these steps:

1. Position the cell pointer on the cell you want to erase.

2. Press / (slash) to display the Main menu.

3. Select Range.

4. Select Erase from the subcommand list (see Figure 11-3).

5. Press Enter. 1-2-3 then removes the contents of the cell and displays the blank cell in the worksheet.

Deleting Rows and Columns You may want to delete an entire row or column on your worksheet. This technique is explained in Lesson 15.

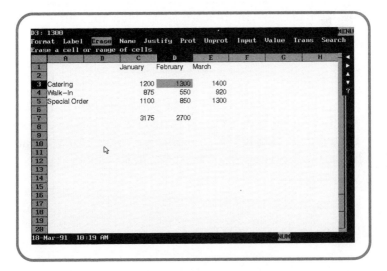

Figure 11-3. Choosing **/R**ange Erase.

In this lesson you've learned to edit and delete cells in the worksheet. You also learned how to recalculate formulas. In the next lesson you'll learn how to format the values and labels in your spreadsheet.

Formatting the Worksheet

In this lesson you'll learn to change the numeric format for portions of the worksheet and for the entire worksheet.

1-2-3 gives you more than one option for formatting the data in your spreadsheet. You can change the format of selected cells (known as *formatting a range*), or you can change the format of the entire worksheet (known as *global formatting*).

Formatting Ranges

You use the **/R**ange **F**ormat command to change the format for a range of cells. Select this command to display the format options in the control panel. Table 12-1 explains each of the options available.

Figure 12-1 shows the addition of another column, Averages, in the sample worksheet. This column includes decimal values. For this example, use the Fixed format to suppress the decimal display and round the fractional values. Take a minute and enter the values shown in Figure 12-1.

Table 12-1. Numeric Formats.

Format	You Enter	1-2-3 Displays
Fixed	23.89	24
Scientific	–32	–3E+02
Currency	1423789	$1,423,789
(Comma)	987654	987,654
General	23.23	23.23
+/–	5	+++++
–	5	———
Percent	.075	75%
Date	@DATE	02-Jan-91
		(91,1,2)
Time	@NOW	10:23 AM
Text	+C3+C4+C5	+C3+C4+C5
Hidden	123	

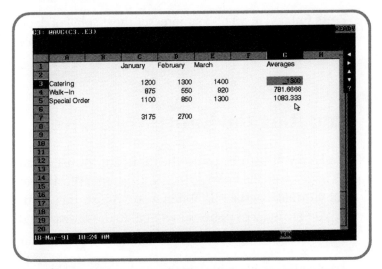

Figure 12-1. The format options available with
/Range Format.

Then follow these steps:

1. Position the cell pointer on cell G3 of the example worksheet.

2. Press / (slash).

3. Select **R**ange.

4. Select **F**ormat.

5. Select **F**ixed.

6. Type 0 at the prompt for the number of decimal places.

7. Press Enter.

8. When prompted to enter the range you want to format, press ↓ twice, highlighting G3..G5.

9. Press Enter. Then 1-2-3 suppresses the display of decimals and rounds the numbers to the nearest integer (see Figure 12-2).

Formatting the Entire Worksheet

1-2-3 gives you the option of changing the format of all values in the worksheet. To do this, you use the **/W**orksheet **G**lobal **F**ormat command. When you choose this command, you see a list of options identical to those displayed when you used **/R**ange Format.

Try displaying all values on the worksheet in **C**urrency format (showing two decimal places):

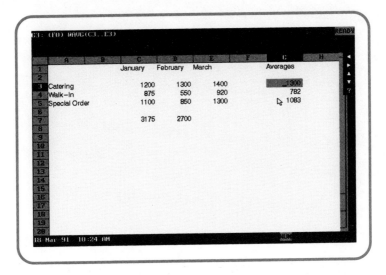

Figure 12-2. The worksheet after range G3..G5 is formatted.

1. Load the sample worksheet, and then press / (slash).

2. Choose Worksheet.

3. Select Global. (This option tells 1-2-3 you want to change all values on the spreadsheet.)

4. Choose Format.

5. Choose Currency.

6. When 1-2-3 asks how many decimal places you want displayed (2 is the default), press Enter.

1-2-3 then formats the values in the worksheet, displaying dollar signs, commas, and decimals at the appropriate places. But, as you can see in Figure 12-3, something unexpected happens. In some of the cells, instead of displaying the numeric values, 1-2-3 displays a string of asterisks (*).

69

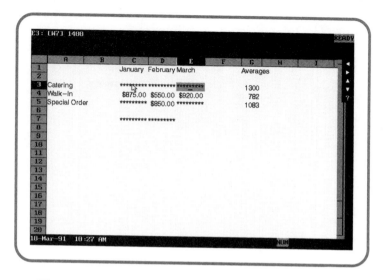

Figure 12-3. Displaying the values in Currency format.

The asterisks are displayed because 1-2-3 doesn't have enough room to display the value in its new Currency format. To display the numbers properly, you need to widen the columns.

Keeping Range Formats Intact When you use /Range Format to change the format of a range, 1-2-3 keeps that setting even when you change the global format of the worksheet.

In this lesson you've learned to work with the format of values in the worksheet. In the next lesson you'll learn how to change column width.

Formatting: Changing Column Width

In this lesson you'll learn how to change the width of columns in your worksheet.

Changing Column Width

1-2-3 automatically displays worksheet columns nine characters wide. If you enter a label that is longer than nine characters, 1-2-3 displays the label anyway; the label appears to cross over into the adjacent cell (if it's empty). When you enter values that are too large for the spreadsheet, however, 1-2-3 displays asterisks in place of the number as a sign to you that you need to widen the columns in the worksheet.

1-2-3 gives you the choice of widening selected columns (using **/W**orksheet **C**olumn **S**et-Width) or widening all columns on the worksheet (using **/W**orksheet **G**lobal **C**olumn-Width)—options similar to the other formatting options.

Changing Individual Column Width

Use the following steps to change the width of one column:

1. Position the cursor in the column whose width you want to change. (Choose column C in the sample worksheet.)

2. Press / (slash).

3. Choose Worksheet.

4. Select Column.

5. Select Set-Width.

6. 1-2-3 then prompts you to enter a column width from 1 to 240 characters. (For this example, type **15**.)

7. Press Enter. 1-2-3 changes the width of the column, and the numbers display correctly (see Figure 13-1).

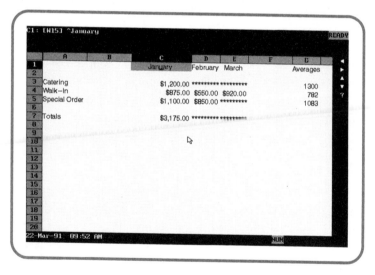

Figure 13-1. Changing the width of one column.

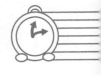

Varying Column Width To get the most out of the space you have on-screen, tailor the width of each column to the size necessary for that column. Use **/W**orksheet **C**olumn **S**et-Width to change the width of each column.

Changing the Width of All Columns

Occasionally, you may want to change the width of all columns on the worksheet. To do this, follow these steps:

1. Open the worksheet.

2. Press / (slash).

3. Choose **W**orksheet.

4. Select **G**lobal.

5. Select **C**olumn-Width.

6. When the `Enter Global Column Width:` prompt is displayed, type a new column width (**10** for our example).

7. Press Enter.

1-2-3 then changes the width of all columns on the worksheet (see Figure 13-2). Now all the numbers in the worksheet display correctly, but the new width pushes the averages column off the screen. Even though you've used the **G**lobal command, 1-2-3 leaves the width of column C set at 15.

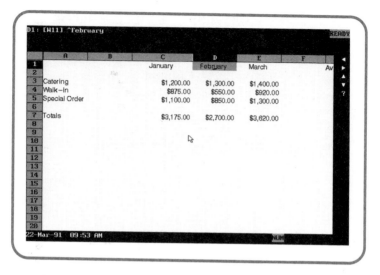

Figure 13-2. Changing column width globally.

Resetting Column Width

After you've modified the columns on the worksheet, you may decide you liked it better the way it was. You can reset the column width to the default width setting by using the **/W**orksheet **C**olumn **R**eset-Width command. Try the following example:

1. Press / (slash).

2. Choose **W**orksheet.

3. Select **C**olumn.

4. Select **R**eset-Width. 1-2-3 then returns the column you specified to the default width.

Changing the Width of a Range of Columns
You can change the width of several columns at one time by using the /Worksheet Column Column-Range command.

Hiding Columns

In some cases you may be working with sensitive data for your use only. 1-2-3 gives you the option of hiding columns in the worksheet so that you control who sees what. To hide a column in the worksheet, follow these steps:

1. Position the cell pointer on the column you want to hide (in this case, in cell C3).

2. Press / (slash).

3. Choose **W**orksheet.

4. Select **C**olumn.

5. Select **H**ide. 1-2-3 displays C3 as the default.

6. Press Enter. 1-2-3 then hides the display of the column (see Figure 13-3). All equations and values in that column are still included in computations performed by the program, so the data is not affected.

Printing Peril If you find that all the columns in your worksheet are not printing, check to see whether you have hidden any columns on the worksheet. Hidden columns do not print.

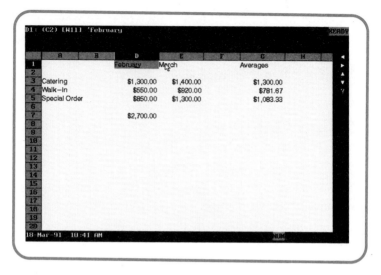

Figure 13-3. Hiding a column.

Redisplaying Columns

To redisplay columns you have hidden on the worksheet, follow these steps:

1. Press / (slash).

2. Choose Worksheet.

3. Select Column.

4. Select Display.

5. When 1-2-3 prompts you to enter the column you want to display, type C3.

6. Press Enter. 1-2-3 then redisplays the column on the worksheet screen.

Lesson 14
Formatting:
Aligning Labels

In this lesson you'll learn to align the text labels in your worksheet.

Understanding Label Alignment

In an earlier lesson you entered column and row labels on your worksheet. When you typed the labels, 1-2-3 automatically aligned the labels along the left edge of the cell (known as *left-justified*).

You can tell 1-2-3 how you want the labels to be formatted by entering a label prefix before the label. Table 14-1 lists the label prefixes.

You can change individual labels or change all labels on the worksheet (global) with the alignment options, which are similar to the other formatting commands.

Table 14-1. Label Prefixes.

Prefix	Description
'	Aligns the label with the left edge of the cell.
"	Aligns the label with the right edge of the cell.
^	Centers the label.
\	Repeats a character you specify.

Changing Alignment of Individual Labels

When you want to change individual labels or a range of cells containing labels, use the **/R**ange Label command. Try the following example:

1. Open a worksheet (use our example, ABC-A.WK1).

2. Press **/** (slash).

3. Choose **R**ange.

4. Select **L**abel.

5. Choose the alignment option you want—**L**eft, **R**ight, or **C**enter. (For the sample worksheet, choose **C**enter.)

6. When 1-2-3 asks, type the range of cells you want to align (**C1..G1** for this example).

7. Press Enter. 1-2-3 then centers the labels in cells C1..G1 (see Figure 14-1).

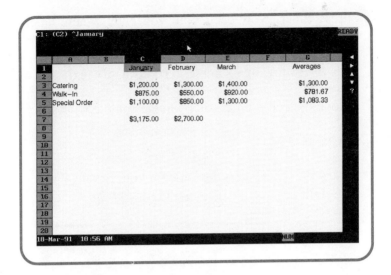

Figure 14-1. Centering labels.

Changing the Default Alignment

1-2-3 allows you to change the default alignment for labels you enter. Change the default alignment—which effects only those labels you enter after changing the default—by using the **/W**orksheet **G**lobal **L**abel-Prefix command.

To change the alignment globally, follow these steps:

1. Press **/** (slash).

2. Select **W**orksheet.

3. Select **G**lobal.

4. Select **L**abel-Prefix.

5. Choose the alignment option you want—**L**eft, **R**ight, or **C**enter. (For this example, choose **R**ight.)

79

6. Press Enter. Now each time you enter a new label, 1-2-3 automatically right-justifies the text.

Try the following example to right-justify text:

1. Move the cell pointer to A7 on the sample worksheet.

2. Type **TOTALS**.

3. Press →. 1-2-3 enters the label for you, placing it along the right edge of the cell (see Figure 14-2).

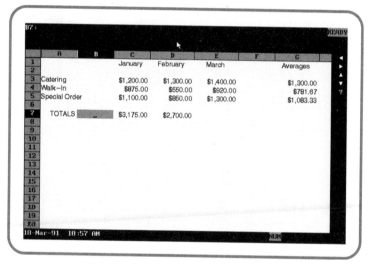

Figure 14-2. Right-justifying labels.

Repeating Labels

You can have 1-2-3 automatically create a label for you by entering a backslash (\) as a label prefix. For example, suppose that you want to add a dashed line just above the TOTALS line. To do this, you could use an equal sign (=)

to display the line in the worksheet. Rather than pressing the equal sign several times, you can have 1-2-3 create the label for you.

To create a repeating label, follow these steps:

1. Position the cell pointer where you want to enter the repeating label (in A6 for this example).

2. Type \=.

3. Press Enter. 1-2-3 fills the cell with = characters, creating the label for you. You can then use the /Copy command to copy the characters across the worksheet (see Figure 14-3).

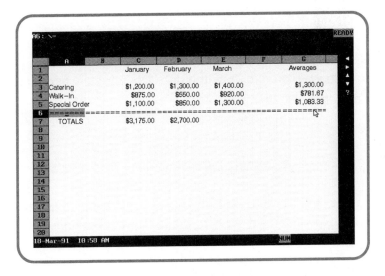

Figure 14-3. Using the \ label prefix.

In this lesson you've learned how to work with the alignment of labels in your worksheet. In the next lesson you'll learn how to enhance the spreadsheet, completing your formatting lessons.

Lesson 15

Working with Rows and Columns

In this lesson you'll learn how to add and remove rows and columns.

Adding Rows and Columns

Occasionally, you'll need to add a row or column in your worksheet to store data you didn't account for when you began the original worksheet. Adding a blank row or column can help organize the look of your worksheet and make it easier for the reader to understand.

Adding Rows and Columns

To add a row or column in the worksheet, use the **/W**orksheet **I**nsert **R**ow or **/W**orksheet **I**nsert **C**olumn commands. Try the following example to add a row to the worksheet:

1. Position the cell pointer in the cell above which you want to insert the row (in the example worksheet, position the cell pointer in A7).

2. Press **/** (slash).

3. Select **W**orksheet.

4. Select Insert.

5. Select Row.

6. When 1-2-3 prompts you to enter a range, press Enter.

1-2-3 inserts the row at the place you specified and modifies the cell addresses used in any formulas that are affected by the change (see Figure 15-1).

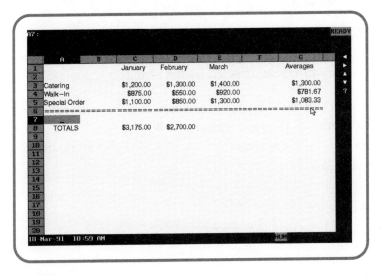

Figure 15-1. Inserting a row.

Inserting Columns You can insert a column in the worksheet by using the /Worksheet Insert Column command.

Deleting Rows and Columns

You can delete a row or column in the worksheet by using the /Worksheet **D**elete **R**ow or /Worksheet **D**elete **C**olumn commands. Try the following example to delete the row you just added:

83

1. Position the cell pointer on the cell in the row you want to delete (in this case, A7).

2. Press / (slash).

3. Select Worksheet.

4. Select Delete.

5. Select Row.

6. When 1-2-3 prompts you to enter a range, press Enter. 1-2-3 then deletes the row you specified and modifies any formulas affected by the change.

In this lesson you've learned to work with rows and columns. In the next lesson you'll learn how you can use Wysiwyg to enhance the look of your 1-2-3 worksheet.

Lesson 16
Using Wysiwyg

In this lesson you'll learn how to use 1-2-3's Wysiwyg add-in to further enhance your spreadsheet.

What Is Wysiwyg?

Wysiwyg stands for "what you see is what you get." When you add this program into 1-2-3, what you see on-screen very closely resembles the printed output you will produce later.

You'll discover numerous features in Wysiwyg that allow you to produce presentation-style printouts. Most importantly, Wysiwyg allows you to see your spreadsheet and graphs on-screen as they will appear in print, complete with different fonts, borders, and a variety of other enhancements.

Loading Wysiwyg

To load the Wysiwyg add-in, follow the steps given in Lesson 7 for loading an add-in program.

Figure 16-1 shows the sample worksheet in normal display. When Wysiwyg is active, the screen display changes. As you can see, there are no grid lines displayed in the worksheet area, and the column letters and row numbers appear differently (see Figure 16-2). Additionally, the values in column G are now visible.

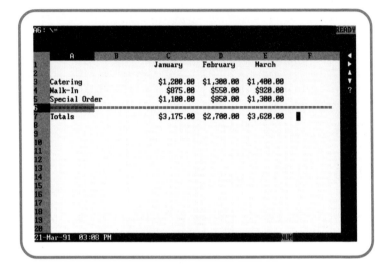

Figure 16-1. Sample worksheet with normal display.

Changing the Look of Text

1-2-3 allows you to change the type you use when you are printing graphs from the 1-2-3 graph printing utility, PrintGraph. Now, with Release 2.3, you can use Wysiwyg to further control the way text looks in your spreadsheets and graph printouts. First, you may need a brief lesson in typography:

A *typeface*, or *type family*, is a particular design of text. Times and Helvetica are two different typefaces.

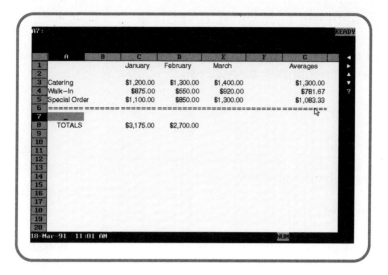

Figure 16-2. The worksheet when Wysiwyg is active.

A *font* is one size and style of a particular type family. Times 10-point Bold type is an example of one font.

The *type style* is the text enhancement feature used. In Times 10-point Bold, boldface is the type style.

A *point* is a unit of measurement indicating the size of the type. A point is equal to 1/72 of an inch.

The *line height* is the amount of space between lines, measured from the base of one character to the bottom of the character directly below it.

A *fixed font* allows exactly the same width for each character.

A *proportional font* gives different characters different widths; that is, a *W* would use more space than an *I*.

87

Changing Fonts and Text Style

To change the font for a particular section of the sample worksheet, follow these steps:

1. Press : (colon).

2. Select F ormat.

3. Select F ont.

4. Press F2.

5. Choose the typeface and size you want by typing the number beside the font or by clicking on that option (in this example, select 2).

6. Press Enter or click OK.

7. When prompted, type the range you want to change (in this case, C1..E1) and press Enter. The worksheet is then displayed with the new font settings in place (see Figure 16-3).

 Changing the Default Font You can change the font 1-2-3 uses as the default font by using :Format Font Replace and then selecting 1 and choosing the new default font.

You can further enhance text by adding boldface or italic text style. To change the style of text, follow these steps:

1. Press : (colon)

2. Select F ormat.

3. Select B old.

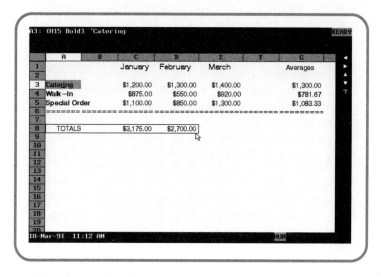

Figure 16-3. The worksheet with the new font, text style, line height, and border.

4. Select Set.

5. Highlight the cell or range of cells you want to change (in this case, cells **A3..A5**) and press Enter. Wysiwyg changes the style of the text as you indicated.

Changing Line Height

You also can use Wysiwyg to change the amount of space used for each row in the worksheet.

1. Press : (colon).

2. Select Worksheet.

3. Choose Row.

4. Choose Set-Height.

5. Select the row or rows you want to change (in this example, A3..A5).

6. Press Enter.

7. Type a new height for the line (the line height is measured in points).

8. Press Enter.

Automatically Setting Line Height You can have Wysiwyg automatically set the line height for you by using **:**Worksheet **R**ow Auto.

Adding Borders Around Text

You can highlight special portions of your spreadsheet by using lines to call attention to particular ranges, columns, or rows. To add a border to a range of worksheet cells, follow these steps:

1. Press **:** (colon).

2. Select **F**ormat.

3. Choose **L**ines.

4. Choose **O**utline.

5. When prompted, enter the range (**A8..D8** for the example worksheet) and press Enter. Wysiwyg adds a border around the range you specified (refer to Figure 16-3).

Adding Lines You can also use the :Format Lines command to add lines around individual cells, underneath cells, to the left or right of cells, or above cells. Additionally, you can use a double line to highlight or outline cells.

Selecting a Worksheet Frame

To modify the frame that surrounds your 1-2-3 worksheet, follow these steps:

1. Press : (colon).

2. Select Display.

3. Choose Options.

4. Choose Frame.

5. Choose Special from the displayed options (1-2-3, Enhanced, Relief, Special, or None). Wysiwyg displays a second set of options. Choose Inches. The top of the frame then changes to a ruler line (see Figure 16-4).

Changing the Worksheet Grid

Wysiwyg also gives you the option of displaying or erasing the grid lines of the worksheet. When you first load Wysiwyg, the grid is turned off. To display the grid, follow these steps:

1. Press : (colon).

2. Select Display.

3. Choose Options.

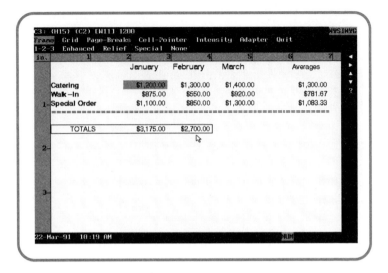

Figure 16-4. The worksheet with the new frame.

4. Choose G rid.

5. Choose Y es. Wysiwyg then displays the grid. To suppress the grid, select :D isplay O ptions G rid N o.

Removing Wysiwyg

When you no longer need Wysiwyg, you may want to
remove it from your computer's memory. Follow the steps
in Lesson 7 for detaching an add-in program.

In this lesson you've learned how to work with the
Wysiwyg program. In the next lesson you'll learn how to
print the worksheet you've created.

Lesson 17

Printing
Worksheets

In this lesson you'll learn to print the worksheet you've created.

Starting the Print Operation

After you've created, edited, formatted, and enhanced your worksheet, you're ready to print. In 1-2-3, you can print to the printer or a disk file. You can print the entire worksheet, current screenful, or a specified range. In most instances, you'll want to print to the printer to get a hard copy printout of the work you've done. (You might print to a file, for example, when you are creating a file that will be printed on another computer.)

When you are ready to initiate the print procedure, follow these steps:

1. Press / (slash).

2. Select Print. 1-2-3 displays the Print menu, giving you the option of printing to a file or to the printer (see Figure 17-1).

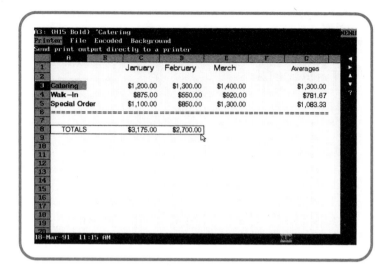

Figure 17-1. The Print menu.

3. Select **P**rinter to send the data to the printer. 1-2-3 displays the subcommands available with the Print menu (see Figure 17-2). Table 17-1 explains each of the commands available in this subcommand list.

4. Select **R**ange.

5. Enter or highlight the range you want to print.

6. Select **A**lign to tell 1-2-3 that the paper is positioned properly.

7. Select **G**o. 1-2-3 then prints the worksheet range you specified.

Stopping Printing If you've forgotten something or you've entered the wrong print range, you can stop printing at any time by pressing Ctrl-Break.

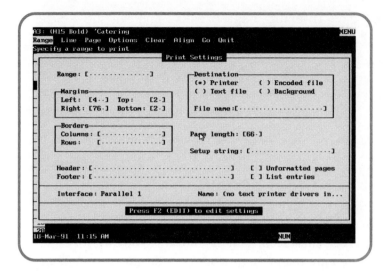

Figure 17-2. The subcommands and Print Settings Dialog box available after selecting **/P**rint **P**rinter.

Table 17-1. Print menu subcommands.

Command	Use to
Range	Specify range to be printed.
Line	Move paper line by line for adjustment.
Page	Adjust alignment page by page.
Options	Change print defaults and enhance printouts.
Clear	Clear previously entered settings.
Align	Tell 1-2-3 that the current position of the paper is the page top.
Go	Begin printing.
Quit	Leave the Print menu.

Inserting Page Breaks You can add a page break within the worksheet by positioning the cell pointer in column A of the row where you want to insert the page break and using the /Worksheet Page command. 1-2-3 inserts the page break characters (¦ ::) at the cell pointer location.

Printing a Screen

You can have 1-2-3 produce a draft quality printout of only the current screen. You might want to do this, for example, if you are planning to work on a different worksheet and want to have a hard copy of the current worksheet to refer to as you're working on the new worksheet. To print the current screen, follow these steps:

1. Display the portion of the worksheet you want to print.

2. Press Shift-PrtSc.

Adding Headers and Footers

1-2-3 automatically reserves six lines for headers and footers in your worksheet printout: three lines for the header, at the top of the page; and three lines for the footer, at the bottom.

To enter a header or footer for the worksheet printout, follow these steps:

1. Press / (slash).

2. Select Print.

3. Choose Printer.

4. Select Range, and enter the range you want to use for the header.

5. Choose Options.

6. Choose Header or Footer.

7. At the prompt, type the text you want to use in the header or footer, for example

   ABC Catering, Inc.

8. After entering the text, choose Quit. 1-2-3 then stores the information with the file and will print the header or footer at print time.

1-2-3 makes things easier for you by giving you a few characters that will substitute dates, page numbers, and alignment information in header and footer lines. Table 17-2 highlights these characters.

Table 17-2. Characters Used in Headers and Footers.

Character	Description
#	Prints page number at character position in header.
@	Prints current date (DD-MM-YY) in header or footer.
|	Centers text following character.
||	Right-justifies text following second character.

Printing a Listing of Cell Contents

Occasionally, you may want to get a printout of the cell contents in your worksheet. This would be particularly important to you, for example, if you have created a series of elaborate formulas that don't seem to be giving you the results you want.

To print the contents of cells on the worksheet, follow these steps:

1. Press / (slash).

2. Select **P**rint.

3. Select **P**rinter.

4. Choose **O**ptions.

5. Choose **O**ther.

6. Choose **A**s-Displayed to print the cell contents as they appear on-screen.

7. Press Esc.

8. Choose **R**ange.

9. Enter the print range.

10. Select **A**lign to align the page.

11. Select **G**o to print the range you've specified. 1-2-3 then produces a vertical list of cell contents, with the cell address listed first, and then the format, width, and actual cell contents of each cell.

Creating a Basic Graph

In this lesson you'll learn to create a simple graph from the data in the 1-2-3 worksheet.

Understanding Graph Types

Graphs help you show trends that you might not see easily from a worksheet full of data. You use graphs to help illustrate the financial information your worksheet has been number-crunching, for example. Table 18-1 highlights 1-2-3's five graph types and provides an example of each.

Table 18-1. 1-2-3 Graph Types.

Type	Description
Line	Shows the trend of data over time. For example, you might graph the sales of a particular department over a period of months.
XY	Compares one range of data to another. For example, you might compare the company's sales totals with the sales of a particular department.

(continued)

Table 18-1. (continued)

Type	Description
Bar	Compares the values in two or more ranges of data. For example, you could use a bar graph to depict the sales of two different products over a period of months.
Stacked-Bar	Shows how individual data items contribute to a total. For example, one bar might represent all of January sales, with segments within that bar showing the sales of individual departments.
Pie	Shows how the values in the series compare to the whole. For example, you might use a pie chart to show annual sales and include a "slice" for each month.

Creating a Bar Graph

For this example, you will produce a bar graph that shows how each of the divisions of ABC Catering did in the first three months of 1991.

When you're ready to create the graph, follow these steps:

1. Press / (slash).

2. Select Graph (see Figure 18-1).

3. Select Type.

4. Choose Bar as the graph type.

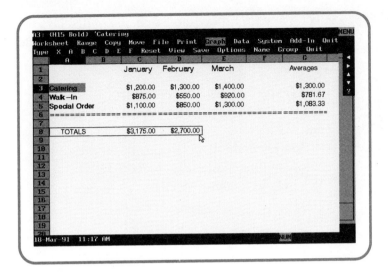

Figure 18-1. The worksheet example, with the **Graph** command highlighted.

5. Select **A** as the first data range you want to graph.

6. In response to the `Enter first data range:` prompt, highlight or type the range (**C3..E3** for the example worksheet) and press Enter.

7. Select **B**.

8. Enter the range (**C4..E4** for the example).

9. Select **C**.

10. Enter the range (**C5..E5** for the example).

11. Choose **X**.

12. Enter the range (**C1..E1** for the example). This tells 1-2-3 which cells to use as labels along the x axis of the graph.

13. Select View to display the graph. 1-2-3 displays the graph you have created (see Figure 18-2). Press Esc to return to the worksheet.

No Graph? Depending on the type of display and the amount of memory you have, you may not see a graph when you are using 1-2-3 in Wysiwyg mode. If this happens, return to the Main menu and select **Add-In Detach WYSIWYG**; then repeat the steps to view your graph.

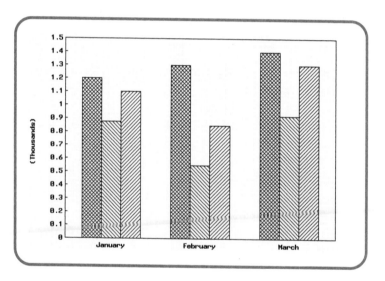

Figure 18-2. The bar graph created from the sample worksheet.

Removing Graph Settings If you've previously created a graph, you may have already entered values for the X, A, B, and C data ranges. To remove the settings so that you can enter new ones, use **/Graph Reset Ranges**.

Creating a Pie Graph

Figure 18-3 shows a sample pie graph. To create it, use the /Graph Type command and choose Pie. You then need only specify an A range (C3..C5) and an X range (A3..A5) because pie charts show only one set of data.

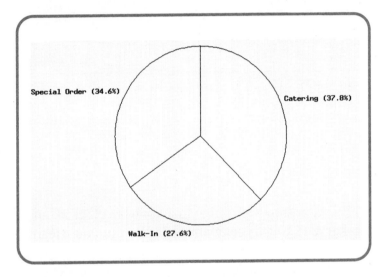

Figure 18-3. A sample pie graph.

In this lesson you've learned about the different types of graphs available and created two basic graphs—a bar graph and a pie graph. In the next lesson you'll learn how to enhance the graphs you've created by using /Graph Options.

Lesson 19
Enhancing Graphs

In this lesson you'll learn how to enhance the graphs you've created.

Enhancing the Graph

This lesson shows you how to add titles, a legend, and a background grid to your graph. Additionally, you'll learn to assign a name to a graph and save a graph in a file separate from the worksheet file.

Adding Titles

When you want to add a title to your graph, use the **/G**raph **O**ptions **T**itles command. Try the following example:

1. Press **/** (slash).

2. Select **G**raph.

3. Select **O**ptions.

4. Select Titles. 1-2-3 displays yet another subcommand line, giving you the option of selecting titles for the first line, second line, x axis, or y axis.

5. Choose First by pressing Enter.

6. After the `Enter first line of graph title:` prompt, type the first line of your title and press Enter.

7. Press Enter again when the Titles command is highlighted.

8. Choose Second.

9. Type another line of text and press Enter.

10. Press F10 to view the graph.

1-2-3 adds the first and second line titles you specified (see Figure 19-1). When you're ready to return to the worksheet, press Esc.

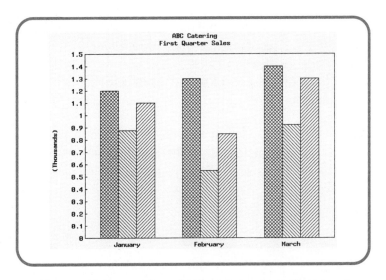

Figure 19-1. Adding titles to the sample bar graph.

Adding a Legend

You can add a legend to your graphs by using the **/G**raph **O**ptions **L**egend command. Follow these steps:

1. Press **/** (slash).

2. Select **G**raph.

3. Select **O**ptions.

4. Select **L**egend.

5. Press Enter.

6. At the `Enter legend for first data range:` prompt, type \ (backslash) and then the address of the cell with the label for the first range of data and press Enter.

7. Highlight **B** and press Enter.

8. Type \ (backslash) and the address of the cell with the label for second range; then press Enter.

9. Repeat steps 7 and 8 to add legends for any other data ranges.

10. Press F10 to view the graph. 1-2-3 then displays the graph complete with titles and legend (see Figure 19-2). Press Esc when you want to return to the worksheet.

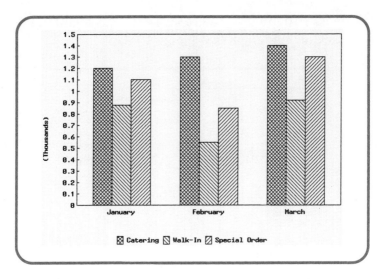

Figure 19-2. The graph with a legend and titles.

Setting a Background Grid

When you first display the graph you create in 1-2-3, the background of the graph is blank. You may, however, want to display a grid so that you can see easily what various data points mean. To set a background grid, follow these steps:

1. Press / (slash).

2. Select Graph.

3. Select Options.

4. Select Grid. 1-2-3 then displays four more options: Horizontal, Vertical, Both, and Clear.

5. Choose an option and press Enter.

107

6. Press F10 to view the graph. 1-2-3 adds a grid to the back of your graph (see Figure 19-3).

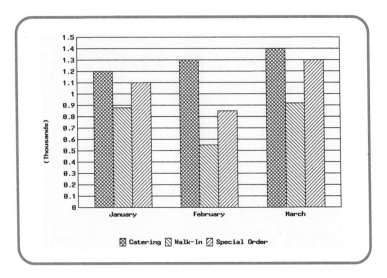

Figure 19-3. Adding a horizontal background grid.

Removing Grid Lines You can remove the grid from the graph by using the /Graph Options Grid Clear command.

Naming a Graph

In some cases you may want to create more than one graph per worksheet. Using numerous graphs allows you to choose the best representation of the data you have created. Assign a name to a graph by following these steps:

1. Press / (slash).

2. Select Graph.

3. Select **N**ame.

4. Select **C**reate.

5. Type a name for the graph, such as **QTR1SLS**, and press Enter. 1-2-3 then assigns the name to the graph.

Saving a Graph

When you save a worksheet using **/Graph S**ave, 1-2-3 saves the graph with the worksheet and gives the file a PIC extension. Sometimes, however, you may want to save a graph independent of the worksheet (such as when you want to print the graph from the PrintGraph program). To do this, you use the **/Graph S**ave command, as follows:

1. Press **/** (slash).

2. Select **G**raph.

3. Select **S**ave.

4. At the `Enter graph file name:` prompt, type a name for the file.

5. Press Enter. 1-2-3 saves the file, and you can access the PrintGraph program to print the graph if you want.

In this lesson you've learned how to enhance the basic graphs you created in the preceding lesson with titles, legends, and grids. You've also learned how to save your graph. In the next lesson you'll learn how to use the PrintGraph program to print your graphs.

Lesson 20
Printing a Graph

In this lesson you'll learn to use 1-2-3's PrintGraph program to print the graphs you've created.

Starting PrintGraph

When you are ready to print the graphs you've created, you'll use another part of 1-2-3, known as the PrintGraph program, to print the files. You start the PrintGraph program from within 1-2-3 by following these steps:

1. Press / (slash).

2. Select System.

3. At the DOS prompt, type **pgraph**.

4. Press Enter. The PrintGraph menu appears (see Figure 20-1).

Memory Problems... If you don't have enough memory available to run PrintGraph while 1-2-3 is active, save your worksheet and exit 1-2-3. Then type **pgraph** at the DOS prompt to start PrintGraph.

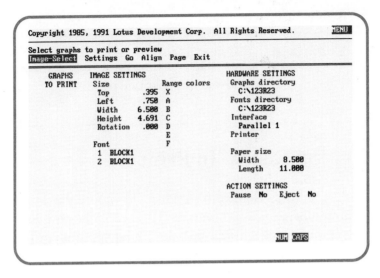

Figure 20-1. The PrintGraph menu.

The PrintGraph Menu

You use the commands in the PrintGraph menu to print the graphs you've created in 1-2-3 and stored as PIC files (see Lesson 19 for information about saving PIC files). Table 20-1 describes the PrintGraph menu commands.

Table 20-1. PrintGraph Commands.

Command	Description
Image-Select	Used to select a graph to be printed.
Settings	Controls the graph size, font, color, and orientation.
Go	Begins printing.
Align	Aligns paper in printer.

(continued)

111

Table 20-1. (continued)

Command	Description
Page	Advances paper one page.
Exit	Exits PrintGraph.

Getting Ready To Print

Use the **S**ettings **H**ardware command to choose the directories for the graphs and fonts, and to specify the port your printer is connected to and the type of printer you are using. (You chose a printer type when you installed 1-2-3; however, if you installed more than one printer, you can choose which to use at this time.) To specify these options:

1. Start PrintGraph, if you haven't already done so.

2. Highlight **S**ettings.

3. Choose **H**ardware.

4. Choose **G**raphs-Directory.

5. Backspace over the default, if necessary, and type the directory where your graphs are stored.

6. Press Enter. PrintGraph then inserts the new graph directory.

7. Select **F**onts-Directory.

8. Backspace over the default and type the directory where fonts are stored. Then press Enter.

9. Choose **P**rinter.

10. When the list of installed printers is displayed, high-
    light the name of the printer you want to use.

11. Press Enter. PrintGraph then inserts the appropriate
    printer in the `Printer Type:` line.

Printing a Simple Graph

When you are ready to print a graph, first make sure your
printer is turned on and ready to go. Then follow these steps:

1. Start PrintGraph by using the steps described earlier.

2. Choose **I**mage-Select. PrintGraph searches the directory you specified using the **G**raph-Directory command and lists the available graphs.

3. Highlight the graph to be printed and press Enter.

4. Select **A**lign.

5. Choose **G**o. 1-2-3 then prints the graph you selected.

Enhancing the Printout

You can change the size of the graph and way the graph is
printed on the page: in portrait mode (8 1/2" by 11") or in
landscape mode (11" by 8 1/2"). You also can change the
fonts used and select different colors for the graph.

Changing Size

When you first start PrintGraph, the program will print your
graph roughly 6 1/2" wide and 4 1/2" tall. The program also
gives these options:

113

- *Full,* in which the graph is rotated 90 degrees and printed to fill the entire page.

- *Half,* the default setting, where the graph is printed half the size of an 8 1/2" by 11" page.

- *Manual,* in which you can customize the size of the graph by entering your own Width and Height settings.

 Controlling Graph Placement Control where the graph prints on the page by setting new Top and Left margins with the Settings Image Size Manual Top (and Left) commands.

To change the size of the graph, follow these steps:

1. Start P rintGraph.

2. Select S ettings.

3. Choose I mage.

4. Choose S ize.

5. Select F ull. PrintGraph changes the settings in the IMAGE OPTIONS portion of the screen. The graph will fill the page and print in landscape (11" by 8 1/2") orientation.

 Adjusting Orientation Change the orientation of the graph by selecting Image Size Manual Rotation and entering **90** for the Rotation setting.

Changing Fonts

You can change the fonts used for graph labels, titles, and legends. To specify a new font, follow these steps:

1. From the PrintGraph menu, select Settings.

2. Choose Image.

3. Choose Font. PrintGraph displays a list of fonts available (see Figure 20-2). Select the number for the type of font you want to change.

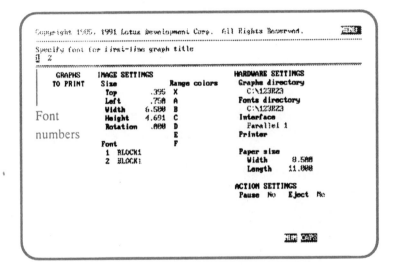

Figure 20-2. Selecting a new font.

4. Highlight the font you want to use, press the space bar, and then press Enter.

5. To choose an additional font, repeat steps 3 and 4.

PrintGraph then updates the screen and stores the new settings with the information used at print time.

Lesson 21
Creating a Simple Database

In this lesson you'll learn to build a simple 1-2-3 database.

What Is a Database?

A *database* is any collection of information that you organize in a certain way. For example, a Rolodex represents one database, while a shoebox full of receipts represents another. Any time you're storing information, you're creating a database.

1-2-3 makes it easy for you to create a database to store a number of important information items, whether you need to record names, addresses, and phone numbers of clients or maintain an elaborate inventory related to your business operations.

Understanding the 1-2-3 Database

The 1-2-3 database doesn't look any different from the worksheet—in fact, you can create the database right in a worksheet file along with your worksheet, or you can create a separate file to store the database.

If you choose to create the database in the same file as a worksheet, however, be sure to choose a section of the worksheet far away from the worksheet data. This keeps any data-manipulation operations from affecting the numbers on your worksheet.

Table 21-1 lists some database terms you'll see in this and the next lessons.

Table 21-1. Database Terms.

Term	Definition
Field	A single information item, such as Address or Phone.
Record	One complete set of fields related to a particular item; for example, if you were creating a client database, one record might consist of Name, Address, City, State, ZIP, and Phone fields.
Database	A file storing a number of records related to a file specific topic; in this example, all client records would be stored in one database file.

Figure 21-1 shows you a sample 1-2-3 database. Within the worksheet structure, one row represents a *record*, and one cell (the intersection of a column and row) shows an individual *field* within a record. The entire block of information represents the database itself. The LASTNAME, ADDRESS, CITY, ST, ZIP, and PHONE labels identify the database fields. The row of information about each client, for example, is a record.

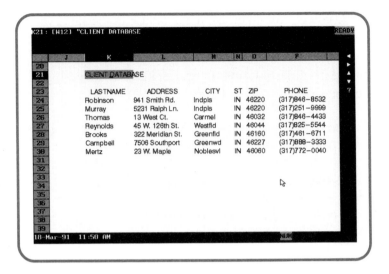

Figure 21-1. A sample database.

Building the Database

There are basically four steps in building a database with 1-2-3:

1. Planning the database.

2. Entering labels.

3. Entering data.

4. Saving the database.

The first step in building the database involves planning. For your own databases, think about what type of information you need to include and in what order. You may find writing out the organization of your database helpful before you enter it on-screen.

118

After you've planned out the database, you're ready to start entering the database labels.

Entering Labels

Before you begin, move the cell pointer to a place on your worksheet far away from any worksheet information you have entered. Enter a label by typing the label you want to use and pressing → to move to the next cell. Repeat this step until you've entered labels for all the fields in your database.

Entering Data

Now that you've got the basic organization of the database, you're ready to enter data. Simply position the pointer on the cell in which you want to add information, type the data, and move the pointer to the next cell. Continue until you've entered all the necessary data.

> **Squashed Data** You may need to widen the columns in order to display all the data in the cells. Lesson 13 explains how to change column width.

Saving the Database

Remember to save your files periodically. Whether you are creating the database as a new file or adding the database into an existing worksheet file, you should save the file as soon as you have entered the labels and the first few records. Use **/F**ile **S**ave to save the file as you would any other spreadsheet file. (For more information about saving files, see Lesson 5.)

In this lesson you'll learn how to sort the data you enter in a database.

Understanding 1-2-3 Sort Operations

Keeping information in a database is pointless unless you have some method of organizing the data. For example, if you have 100 records in a database but have no way of alphabetizing the clients' names, the only way you can locate a specific record is to scroll through the list until you find the one you want.

1-2-3 gives you several options for sorting the data in the database. By sorting within a certain field (known as a *key field*), you can organize the data, for example, by LASTNAME, CITY, or ZIP CODE. In fact, you can sort the data based on any of the fields in the database, but some—like PHONE—would be useless in a sort operation.

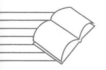

Key Fields Use *key fields* to specify the sort operation. For example, to sort all the records in your database alphabetically by LASTNAME, the LASTNAME field is the key field.

1-2-3 can sort on one or two key fields. An example of a one-key sort would be alphabetizing all records by LASTNAME. A two-key sort would be first sorting the records by CITY (so that clients from various cities are lumped together and the cities are listed in alphabetical order) and then alphabetizing the records (within the CITY sort) by LASTNAME. In this case, the key fields are CITY and LASTNAME.

Sorting on One Key Field

For this example, you'll alphabetize the client records according to LASTNAME. First, make sure the database portion of the sample worksheet is displayed on-screen (see the example in Figure 22-1). To sort the records, follow these steps:

1. Type / (slash).

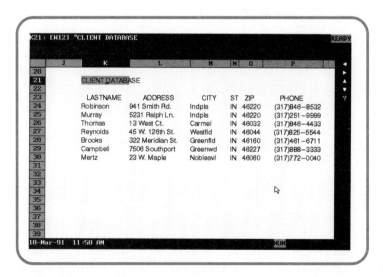

Figure 22-1. The sample database.

2. Select **D**ata.

3. Select **S**ort (see Figure 22-2).

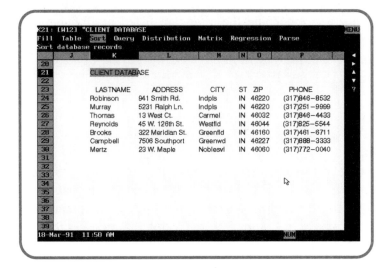

Figure 22-2. The Data menu, with the **S**ort command highlighted.

4. Select **D**ata-Range.

5. 1-2-3 displays the `Enter Data Range:` prompt. Highlight the cells or type the cell addresses of the range you want to sort. Include only the data in the range to be sorted—not the labels. (For the example, type **K24..P30**.) Press Enter.

6. Select **P**rimary-Key. (This tells 1-2-3 that you are choosing the key field.)

7. Move the cell pointer to any entry in the field you want to use as the key field (for the example database, move the cell pointer to cell K24).

8. Press Enter. 1-2-3 displays the Sort Settings dialog box (see Figure 22-3).

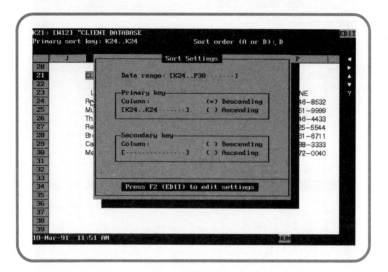

Figure 22-3. The Sort Settings dialog box.

9. Type **A** if you want to choose **A**scending order or **D** to choose **D**escending order.

10. Select **G**o. 1-2-3 then sorts the database according to the settings you have chosen.

Figure 22-4 shows the records organized alphabetically according to the LASTNAME field.

Sorting on Two Key Fields

As mentioned earlier, 1-2-3 can sort on more than one key field. In the example database, the records are sorted first by CITY and then alphabetically by LASTNAME. Try the following example to sort on two key fields:

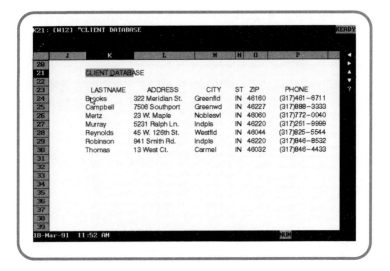

Figure 22-4. The sample database, sorted by the LASTNAME field.

1. Type / (slash).

2. Select Data.

3. Select Sort.

4. Select Data-Range.

5. 1-2-3 then displays the Enter Data Range: prompt. Highlight the cells or type the cell addresses of the range you want to sort. Again, include only the data— not the labels—in the range to be sorted. (For this example, type K24..P30.) Press Enter.

6. Select Primary-Key. (This tells 1-2-3 that you are choosing the first key field.)

7. Move the cell pointer to an entry in the field you want to use as the key field (CITY in this example).

8. Choose **A**scending or **D**escending order.

9. Select **S**econdary-Key. (This tells 1-2-3 that you're selecting the second key field.)

10. Move the cell pointer to an entry in another field. (For example, choose **LASTNAME**.)

11. Choose **A**scending or **D**escending order.

12. Back at the Sort menu, select **G**o. 1-2-3 sorts the records.

Figure 22-5 shows the example database sorted first by CITY and then by LASTNAME.

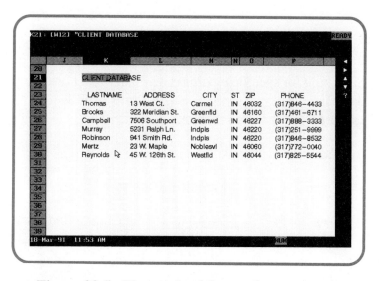

Figure 22-5. The result of the two-key sort.

In this lesson you've learned how to sort the records in your database. In the next lesson you learn how to search for specific records in the database.

Lesson 23

Searching for Data

In this lesson you'll learn how to find specific records in the database.

Understanding Search Operations

Searching for specific records is a primary function of any database. Table 23-1 gives some terms you'll need to explore 1-2-3's search feature.

Table 23-1. Terms Used in Search Operations.

Term	Definition
Data query	Requests the database to find a specific record or group of records.
Criterion range	Contains the information on which you base the search.
Output range	Is the cell range where 1-2-3 places the records it extracts or copies from the database.

Determining the Criterion Range

Suppose, for example, that you want to find all records that have Greenfld entered in the CITY field of a database. The first step is to set up a criterion range so that 1-2-3 knows what information to look for. To create the criterion range, follow these steps:

1. Move to a place on the worksheet away from the database and the worksheet (for this example, use K45).

2. Type **CRITERION RANGE** and press ↓.

3. Type the name of the field you want to search (for example, type **CITY**).

4. Press ↓ again.

5. Type the information you want to search for (for this example, type **Greenfld**) and press ↓. Your criterion range should look like the one in Figure 23-1.

6. Next, select **/Data Query**. The Query Settings dialog box shown in Figure 23-2 is displayed.

7. Press F2.

8. Type **I**.

9. In the Input range: line, type the cell addresses of the database or point to the records you want to include in the search. (For this example, type **K23..P30**.)

10. Press Tab to move to the Criteria range: line.

11. Type the range containing the criterion field name and data (**K46..K47** in the example).

127

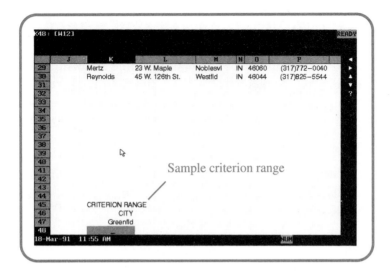

Figure 23-1. The search criterion range.

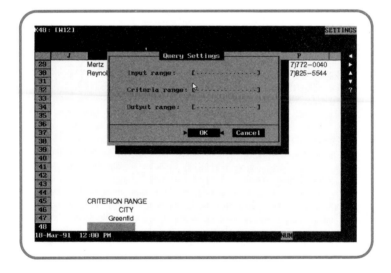

Figure 23-2. The Query Settings dialog box.

12. Press Enter; then press Esc.

13. Choose /D ata Q uery F ind. 1-2-3 then locates the first record that matches the information you specified in the criterion range (see Figure 23-3).

Finding Additional Records Press ↓ to move to the next record matching the search information. To end the search, press Esc.

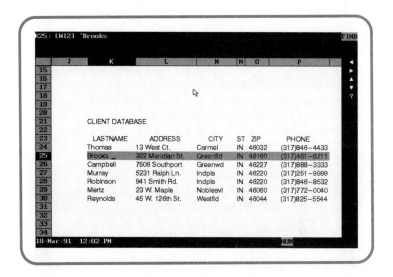

Figure 23-3. Finding the record with the information specified.

Extracting Records

1-2-3 gives you the option of extracting a group of records— that is, you can copy a group of records from the database and place the copy in another range on the worksheet. To extract a group of records, follow these steps:

1. Select the criterion range.

2. Move to a point on the worksheet below the criterion range (in this case, K50).

3. Type **OUTPUT RANGE** and press ↓.

4. Copy the field names in the first line of the database and place the copy just below OUTPUT RANGE (cell K51, for example). Your output range would look like the one in Figure 23-4.

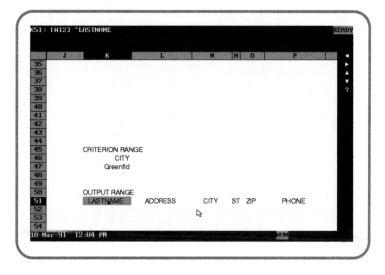

Figure 23-4. Setting up the output range.

5. Select /Data Query Output.

6. When prompted, highlight the row containing the field names in the output range and press Enter.

7. Select Extract.

8. Press Enter. 1-2-3 copies all records that meet the information in the criterion range and places them in the output range (see Figure 23-5).

In this lesson you've learned some basics of searching for information in the 1-2-3 database. The search process can be somewhat complicated, and, for that reason, you may want to consult *The First Book of Lotus 1-2-3 Release 2.3* to learn more about this subject.

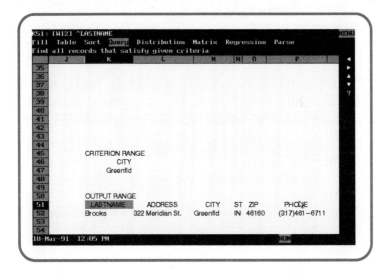

Figure 23-5. Performing an extract operation.

This lesson concludes your course through the *10 Minute Guide to Lotus 1-2-3 Release 2.3*. Following this lesson, you will find a Table of Features and a Table of Functions designed to help you learn more about the aspects of the program not covered fully in these lessons.

Table of Functions

The following table lists some of the most often-used functions in 1-2-3 Release 2.3. For a complete listing of @functions, see *The First Book of Lotus 1-2-3 Release 2.3*, Second Edition.

Function	Description	Syntax	Example
@ABS	Finds absolute value	@ABS(number)	@ABS(–123.45)
@AVG	Finds average	@AVG(range)	@AVG(C3..C5)
@COUNT	Counts number of cells in a range	@COUNT(range)	@COUNT (A7..N9)
@CTERM	Compounding periods	@CTERM (interest, future, present)	@CTERM(.10/12, 40000, 32000)
@DATE	Calculates the date number	@DATE(year, month, day)	@DATE (1991,23,2)
@FV	Finds future value of an investment	@FV(payments, interest, term)	@FV(1100,.075, 24)
@IRR	Finds internal rate of return	@IRR(guess, range)	@IRR(.15, A3..A9)

Function	Description	Syntax	Example
@LN	Finds natural logarithm	@LN(number)	@LN(3)
@LOG	Determines logarithm	@LOG	@LOG(1000)
@MAX	Finds largest value	@MAX(range)	@MAX(C3..D5)
@MIN	Finds smallest value	@MIN(range)	@MIN(V23..X30)
@NOW	Returns today's date	@NOW	@NOW
@PI	Returns Pi	@PI	@PI
@RAND	Returns a random number	@RAND	@RAND
@RATE	Finds interest rate	@RATE(future, present, term)	@RATE(23000, 18000,50)
@ROUND	Rounds number	@ROUND (number)	@ROUND (343.358)
@STD	Finds standard deviation	@STD(range)	@STD(F10..K10)
@SUM	Totals values	@SUM(range)	@SUM(A3..D10)
@TIME	Calculates based on time	@TIME(hour, minutes, seconds)	@TIME(23,9,0)

Table of Features

Feature	Description	To Start
Auditor	Add-in that lets you analyze worksheet formulas.	/Add-In Attach **AUDITOR.ADN**.
Databases	Create databases within 1-2-3's column and row format; use /**D**ata commands to sort, find, and report on information	Enter data in spread sheet; use /**D**ata commands to work with database information.
Formulas	Calculate data using numbers, text, or formulas.	Enter +, −, @, (, or $; then specify cell addresses or values to be used in the equation.
@Functions	Built-in equations you use in formulas to calculate cell values.	Enter the @function name, (, the cell addresses, and a closing).
Graphs	Display trends in data by producing graphs (bar, pie, line, stacked bar, mixed, high-low-close, or XY).	Enter data in the worksheet; then use /**G**raph commands to select ranges, choose options, and view the graph.
Labels	Text you use to label the data in the worksheet.	Enter the label as you want it to appear.

Feature	Description	To Start
Linking files	Link data in a second worksheet to data in the current worksheet.	Enter +, the file name in double angle brackets (<< and >>), and then the cell to which you want to link the file. For example, +<<ABC.WK1>>C23 links the file ABC.WK1 to cell C23.
Macros	Automate 1-2-3 operations by recording repetitive keystrokes.	Create the macro; then run it by pressing Alt-F3.
Macro Library Manager	Add-in feature that allows you to create a library of macros you use often.	/Add-In Attach MACROMGR.ADN.
Ranges	A block of adjacent cells; used in formulas or 1-2-3 operations (such as /Copy or /Move).	Type or point to the first cell address in the range; then type two periods (..), and type or point to the ending address.
Undo	Lets you cancel the most recent operation or settings changes.	/Worksheet Global Default Other Undo Enable; then press Alt-F4.
Viewer	Add-in that lets you view file contents without retrieving them.	/Add-In Attach VIEWER.ADN.
Wysiwyg	Add-in that allows you to see the worksheet as it appears in print, with different options for print and display enhancements such as fonts, shading, frames, and borders.	/Add-In Attach WYSIWYG.ADN.

DOS Primer

This section highlights some of the DOS procedures you will use during your work with this program.

DOS is your computer's Disk Operating System. It functions as a go-between program that lets the various components of your computer system talk with one another. Whenever you type anything using your keyboard, whenever you move your mouse, whenever you try to print a file, DOS interprets the commands and coordinates the task. The following sections explain how to run DOS on your computer and what you can expect to see.

Starting DOS

If you have a hard disk, DOS is probably already installed on the hard disk. When you turn on your computer, DOS automatically loads, and you can begin using your computer. If you don't have a hard disk, however, you must insert the startup disk that contains the DOS program files into the floppy disk drive before starting your computer:

1. Hold the disk by its label, with the label facing up, and insert the opposite end into the floppy drive.

2. If the floppy drive has a door, close the door, and start your computer. Your computer loads DOS into an electronic storage area called *RAM* (Random Access Memory), where DOS stays until you turn off the computer.

3. If you are asked to type the date, type it in the format requested. For example, if DOS prompts you to type the date in the format MM-DD-YY (Month-Day-Year), type something like **02-24-91**, and press Enter.

4. If DOS requests it, type the time in the requested format. For example, if DOS prompts you to type the time in the format HH:MM:SS (Hour:Minute:Second), type something like **08:30:05** and press Enter.

5. When the indicator light next to the floppy drive goes off, you can remove the DOS disk from the drive.

Changing Disk Drives

Once DOS is loaded, you should see a *prompt* (also known as the DOS prompt) on screen that looks something like A:> or A> (or C:> or B:>). This prompt tells you which disk drive is currently active. If you have a hard disk, the disk is usually labeled C. (Most computers have only one hard disk, but it may be treated as several disks: C, D, E, F, and so on.) The floppy disk drives, located on the front of your computer, are drives A and B. If you have only one floppy drive, it's usually A. If you have two floppy drives, the top or left drive is usually A, and the bottom or right drive is B. Activate a different drive at any time by:

1. Make sure there's a formatted disk in the drive you want to activate.

2. Type the letter of the drive followed by a colon. For example, type a:.

3. Press Enter. The DOS prompt changes to show that the drive you selected is now active.

Making Backups of the 1-2-3 Program Disks with DISKCOPY

Before you install Lotus 1-2-3 Release 2.3 on your hard disk, you should make *backup copies* of the original program disks. By using backups to install or run the program, you avoid the risk of damaging the original disks.

Obtain six blank 5.25" double-sided double-density disks or three blank 3.5" double-sided double-density disks. The type of disk should be marked on the package. Because the DISKCOPY command copies the entire disk, you don't have to format the blank disks before you begin.

1. Change to the drive containing the DOS program files.

2. If the DISKCOPY file is in a separate directory, change to that directory as explained earlier. For example, if the file is in the C:\DOS directory, type **cd\dos** at the C : > prompt, and press Enter.

3. Type diskcopy a: a: or diskcopy b: b:, depending on which drive you're using to make the copies.

4. Press Enter. A message appears, telling you to insert the source diskette into the floppy drive.

5. Insert the original Lotus 1-2-3 Release 2.3 disk you want to copy into drive A and press Enter. DOS copies the disk into RAM. When DOS is done copying the

original disk, a message appears telling you to insert the target diskette into the floppy drive.

6. Insert one of the blank disks into the floppy drive, and press Enter. DOS copies the disk from RAM onto the blank disk. When the copying is complete, a message appears, asking if you want to copy another diskette.

7. Remove the disk from the drive, and label it with the same name and number and the original disk.

8. If you need to copy another original disk, press Y and go back to step 5. Continue until you copy all the original disks.

9. When you're done copying disks, type N when asked if you want to copy another disk.

10. Put the original disks back in their box and store them in a safe place.

Formatting Floppy Disks

The first step in preparing floppy disks to store programs and data is formatting the disks.

What Is Formatting? It creates a map on the disk that tells DOS where to find the information you store on the disk. You cannot place any programs or data of any kind on a new disk before the disk is formatted. Formatting also erases any information on a diskette. *Do not* format your hard disk drive, because formatting erases all programs and information on the hard disk.

1. Turn on your computer.

2. Change to the drive and directory that contains your DOS files. For example, if your DOS files are in C:\DOS, type **cd\DOS** at the C> prompt and press Enter.

3. Insert the blank floppy disk you want to format in the A: or B: drive.

4. Type **FORMAT A:** or **FORMAT B:** and press Enter. The system will tell you to insert the disk (which you've already done).

5. Press Enter. The system then begins formatting the disk. When the format is complete, the system asks whether you want to format another.

6. Type **Y** if you want to format additional disks, and then repeat all steps. Otherwise, type **N** to quit.

Labeling Disks While the disk is being formatted, you can write the labels for the disks. Write on the labels before you attach them to the diskettes. (If you've already placed the labels on the diskettes, write on the labels using a felt-tip pen. The hard point of a ball-point pen can damage the surface of a diskette.)

Working with Directories

Because hard drives hold much more information than floppy drives, hard drives are usually divided into directories. For example, when you install Lotus 1-2-3, the Installation program suggests that you copy the Lotus 1-2-3 program files to a directory called *123R23* on drive C. This directory then branches off from the *root directory* of drive C, keeping all the 1-2-3 program files separate from all the other files on drive C. Directories can contain subdirectories as well, branching off as branches of a tree would.

Making Directories

To create a directory, you use the **MD** (Make Directory) command. Follow these steps:

1. Change to the drive that you want to have the directory.

2. At the DOS prompt, type md\ *directoryname*. (Substitute the name for the directory you are creating in place of *directoryname*.)

3. Press Enter. The directory now exists off the root directory. If you want to create a subdirectory off a directory, type the *directoryname*, a backslash and then a *subdirectoryname*, and press Enter.

Note: You do not need to create a directory to run 1-2-3; the installation program does this for you. You can create additional directories to store your data files, however.

Moving to a Directory

You need to be able to move from directory to directory. To change directories, you use the **CD** (Change Directory) command:

1. Change to the drive that contains the directory.

2. At the DOS prompt, type cd\ *directoryname*. (For example, type cd\123R23.) The backslash (\) you type tells DOS to begin at the root directory and move to the directory you specified under the root. Use the backslash

to separate all directories and subdirectories in a command line. For example, to move to a subdirectory of a directory, the command line would look like this:

```
CD\directoryname\subdirectoryname
```

This command line specifies a complete *path* to the subdirectory.

3. Press Enter.

Displaying Directory Contents

To see which files are stored in a directory, use the **DIR** (Directory) command.

1. Change to the drive and directory whose contents you want to view.

2. Type **dir** and press Enter. A list of files appears.

If the list is too long to fit on the screen, it scrolls off the top. You can view the entire list by typing **/p** (pause) or **/w** (wide) after the **DIR** command. If you type **dir/p**, DOS displays one screenful of files; you can see the next screen by pressing Enter. If you type **dir/w**, DOS displays the list across the screen, fitting many more file names on screen.

Working with Files

DOS also includes commands you can use to work with the files you create. This section briefly introduces the procedures for copying, deleting, and renaming files.

Copying Files

To copy files using DOS, use the **COPY** command:

1. Move to the directory that stores the file (or files) you want to copy.

2. Type the command line:

   COPY filename1 drive:\directoryname\filename2

   In this command line, *filename1* is the name of the existing file you want to copy, *drive:\directoryname* is the drive and directory you want to copy the file to, and *filename2* is the new name you want to give the copy of the file. If you want to create a copy of the file in the same drive or directory, you can omit the path (*drive:\directoryname*) before *filename2*.

3. Press Enter. DOS copies the file and places the copy in the current directory.

Deleting Files

To delete files using DOS, you use the **DELETE** (or DEL) command:

1. Move to the directory that stores the file you want to delete.

2. Type the command line:

   DEL filename

3. Press Enter.

4. When DOS asks you for confirmation, type Y. DOS deletes the file.

Renaming Files

You use the **RENAME** (or REN) command to rename files in DOS:

1. Move to the directory that stores the file you want to rename.

2. Type the command line:

   REN filename1 filename2

   In this command line, *filename1* is the name of the existing file, and *filename2* is the new name you want to assign to the file.

3. Press Enter. DOS renames the file and keeps it in the current directory.

For more information about using DOS commands, see *The First Book of MS-DOS.*

Index

M-N

O-P

Q-R